HOW TO ...

enhance the mental health and emotional wellbeing of primary children with SEN

Dr Melanie Forster

Grateful thanks to the children from the North Yorkshire schools who provided wonderful illustrations for inclusion in this book, and their supportive parents and teachers.

How to enhance the mental health and emotional wellbeing of primary children with SEN

ISBN: 978-1-85503-597-3

© Dr Melanie Forster 2015
Illustrations by Ivana Svabic/Beehive Illustration

This edition published 2015
10 9 8 7 6 5 4 3 2 1

Printed in the UK by Page Bros (Norwich) Ltd
Designed and typeset by Andy Wilson for Green Desert Ltd

LDA, 2 Gregory Street, Hyde, Cheshire, SK14 4HR

www.ldalearning.com

CONTENTS

PREFACE

Childhood represents a key time in an individual's life where foundations for positive and successful development and functioning are laid down. The skills learnt during this time can significantly impact upon the level of wellbeing, success and achievement experienced as an adolescent and on through into adulthood (DfE, 2001). There is a strong evidence base showing the importance of positive influences from early stimulating and supportive environments alongside caring and nurturing relationships, highlighting how early and middle childhood represents a profoundly important window of opportunity for a child's learning and growth (Daniel & Wassell, 2003). For children with special educational needs (SEN) this is especially true, as children with complex learning needs often require additional support from within their environment in order to reach everyday developmental milestones that many other children take in their stride.

Providing high quality and effective services to vulnerable children and their families within a climate of austerity and economic challenge creates a particularly difficult context in which many practitioners work. More than ever, service providers have to demonstrate their impact in tangible ways whilst proving that they are also 'good value for money', so finding more effective ways of working with fewer resources is the working context for many (Hopwood & Pharoah, 2012). There is an increasing recognition of the important role schools can play in promoting and facilitating the emotional health of children (DfE, 2014). Knowing how best to support the emotional wellbeing of primary-aged children is not always easy, yet it is becoming an increasingly integral part of many practitioners' everyday practice. Many children and young people, especially those with SEN, experience growing up as a confusing and emotionally challenging time. Children with SEN are known to have an increased risk of experiencing significant emotional distress and many go on to develop a mental health disorder (Emmerson & Hatton, 2007). Alongside specialist mental health service providers, practitioners working within educational and social care settings need to provide effective emotional support for this group of vulnerable children.

This book will provide a framework for developing an effective provision of emotional support and intervention for those children identified as 'at risk' of developing mental health problems, as well as guide appropriate school provision for children already identified as having emotional and mental health difficulties. It will highlight strategies based upon best-practice recommendations for universal provision to enhance emotional resilience and introduce a framework for developing individual targeted interventions. This book will also help practitioners see how their individual input and provision sits within a wider context of support as part of a whole-school commitment to strengthening emotional health. Everyone who works with children with SEN is committed to providing the best support they can to help those children achieve their greatest potential. By strengthening practitioners' knowledge about and skills in dealing with children's mental health and emotional wellbeing, we will ensure that promoting the emotional needs of children with SEN will become 'everyone's business' (as advocated by HM Government UK in 2011). This book will undoubtedly help practitioners meet this goal.

Please note that while every effort has been made to use inclusive language, the term 'parent' has been used for the sake of brevity in many cases, but can also refer to a child's carer. Similarly, 'school' can also refer to any primary setting.

CHAPTER 1
The national and local context for supporting children with SEN

The current picture

Today's children and young people are increasingly exposed to a vast array of pressures and demands which can have a significant impact upon their emotional wellbeing. A report by Relate (Faulkner, 2011) indicated that within a typical class of 30 pupils, a significant number will have experienced notable emotional distress by the age of 16, with a third having seen their parents separate and a quarter having experienced bullying. Around 10% will have a diagnosable mental health illness. Many of these difficulties begin in early childhood and develop throughout the teenage years.

Particular groups of children within our society are more at risk of developing mental health difficulties than others. Children with special educational needs (SEN) are an identified group who are particularly vulnerable to developing a mental health illness. A study by Emmerson & Hatton (2007) which looked at the prevalence of emotional and mental health issues in children and young people found that those with SEN were six times more likely to develop mental health problems than those without SEN.

The term 'special educational needs' is used when a child has significant developmental or learning needs, a disability or health condition which impacts markedly upon their ability to achieve and learn and requires their care, support and educational provision to be adapted in some way. In England, it is estimated that approximately 18% of all pupils within primary and secondary education are considered to have SEN (DfE, 2014b).

Approximately 25% of all children and young people between the ages of five and 16 years have emotional or mental health difficulties. Whilst the majority have emotional difficulties that are overcome with appropriate support, 10% have significant mental health needs that require specialist input.

The most commonly seen mental health difficulties in children link to issues with conduct and behaviour, followed by those associated with emotional distress (including depression and anxiety). A small but concerning number of children and young people have more than one mental health diagnosis and require significant support and therapeutic intervention.

DfE, 2014b

Some children's special learning needs may be specific and targeted within one or two main areas of functioning or development. With additional support and focused intervention, many of these children are able to progress throughout school successfully and achieve their aspirations and goals. However, for other children with more complex or profound difficulties, their ability to learn is affected more globally and impacts upon all or most areas of their development and functioning. These children are likely to need lifelong support and few will develop full independence when living as adults. The generic term 'special educational needs' therefore describes a wide range of disabilities and difficulties that can include:

- ✿ physical or sensory impairments

- ✿ speech or language and communication difficulties

- ✿ cognitive disabilities (ranging from specific learning needs to profound and complex learning difficulties)

- ✿ medical health conditions

- ✿ emotional, social and behavioural difficulties.

In recent years, there has been a move away from defining children's needs simply in terms of a diagnostic label and delivering services based around diagnostic criteria, to considering need relating to how a child's difficulties impact upon their functioning, wellbeing and development. Although it can be valuable to have an accurate understanding of a child's level of difficulties in relation to a diagnosis (such as autism, developmental co-ordination disorder (DCD)/ dyspraxia or mild learning disability), it is of vital importance to consider how the difficulties the child experiences are affecting their overall development and functioning with reference to their:

It is difficult to obtain a fully accurate picture regarding the level of difficulty children with SEN across the UK experience. A recent DfE statistical analysis report indicates that approximately 18% of all pupils have SEN. In state-funded primary schools, the three most common types of SEN are speech, language and communication needs (31%), moderate learning difficulties (19%) and emotional and social difficulties (18%). In special schools, the three most common types of SEN recorded were severe learning difficulties (25%), autism spectrum disorders (22%) and moderate learning difficulties (17%).

DfE, 2014b

- ✿ social, emotional and mental health

- ✿ speech, communication, relationships and interactional skills

- ✿ cognitive learning and acquisition of skills development

- ✿ sensory, physical health and medical needs.

(DfE & DH, 2015)

In reality, a child's learning and development lies upon a continuum of skills and abilities. All children, including those with SEN, fall somewhere along the continuum. Learning difficulties or disabilities are often categorised according to level of need across some or all aspects of development and functioning. This is a useful way of understanding presenting need and helps inform the type of intervention and help required in order to better support a child's development.

Specific learning needs   Mild learning needs   Moderate learning needs   Severe learning needs   Profound learning needs

Special needs continuum (Mansell, 2010)

The SEN learning continuum ranges from specific and focused needs, which impact upon only one particular aspect of a child's development, through to global, profound and often highly complex needs, which often impact upon all or most areas of a child's learning and functioning.

Recent legislative reform

In recent years, the UK government has looked to improve the life outcomes of children and young people with SEN and disabilities through a series of policies and national reforms. This culminated in the Children and Families Act (2014), which looked to improve and align support and services for children and young people with SEN to ensure these youngsters are given the very best opportunities and experiences to enable them to develop to their greatest potential. Additionally, a new SEND Code of Practice (2015) was introduced, containing the statutory guidance on the procedures, policies and duties that related to Part 3 of the Children and Families Act. This section of the Act sets out the general principles and responsibilities local authorities (LAs) and other services must undertake in their support of children with SEN and disabilities. Both documents highlight a number of important developments from previous governmental policies, including:

- ⚙ A new timescale of input and responsibility for all organisations with a statutory duty to support and protect children and young people with SEN and disabilities from birth until the age of 25 years.

- ⚙ Introduction of the Education, Health and Care Plan (EHC) as a new assessment process to consider complex needs. This has replaced statements of educational need and learning difficulty assessments (LDAs) and will form a more co-ordinated and integrated assessment of presenting concerns.

- ⚙ More emphasis upon multi-agency co-ordination and collaboration across education, health and social care in order to provide a more joined-up and supportive network of professional care for a child or young person and their family.

- ⚙ A need for all LAs to make explicit the full range of services available within their community in the form of a local offer (LO), to help families become better informed and more in control of the choices and service options influencing their child's care.

- ⚙ A need for children or young people and their parents to be given greater opportunities to influence and participate in decisions affecting the support they receive, including (where appropriate) direct input into financial budget allocation.

- ⚙ A greater recognition of the profile of social, emotional and mental health difficulties. This is now identified as one of four aspects of development and functioning that organisations could consider commissioning and delivering services around. (This is in addition to communication and interaction, cognition and learning, and sensory and physical needs.)

Highlighting the importance of considering and supporting the emotional and mental health needs of children with SEN in statutory legislation helps emphasise the significant role mental health can play in impacting (both positively and negatively) upon other aspects of a child's development. It ensures that all practitioners consider the emotional wellbeing and mental health of children with SEN as part of their daily input, everyday routines and general provision of care.

The Children and Young People's Health Outcomes Forum reviewed the six identified objectives of the *No health without mental health* government strategy, which aims to build emotional resilience and positive mental health across the lifespan (HM Government UK, 2011). The group modified the lifespan objectives to relate more closely to outcomes for children and young people in order to form an agreed set of principles for all professionals working with children to aim for.

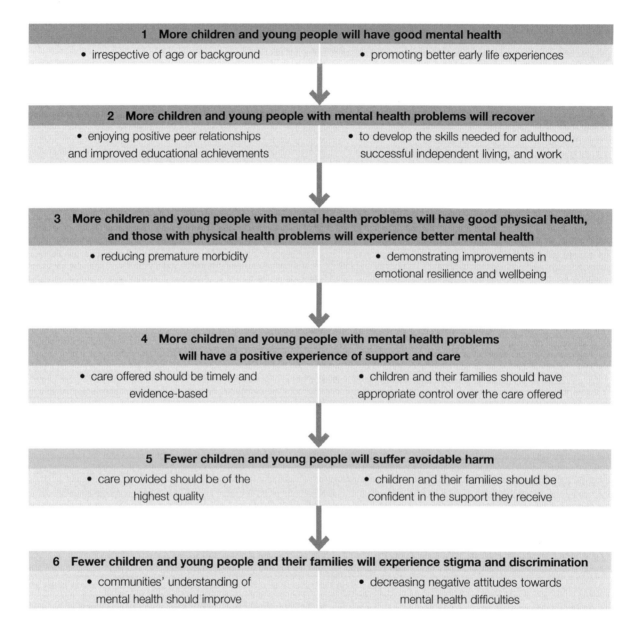

1   More children and young people will have good mental health
- irrespective of age or background
- promoting better early life experiences

2   More children and young people with mental health problems will recover
- enjoying positive peer relationships and improved educational achievements
- to develop the skills needed for adulthood, successful independent living, and work

3   More children and young people with mental health problems will have good physical health, and those with physical health problems will experience better mental health
- reducing premature morbidity
- demonstrating improvements in emotional resilience and wellbeing

4   More children and young people with mental health problems will have a positive experience of support and care
- care offered should be timely and evidence-based
- children and their families should have appropriate control over the care offered

5   Fewer children and young people will suffer avoidable harm
- care provided should be of the highest quality
- children and their families should be confident in the support they receive

6   Fewer children and young people and their families will experience stigma and discrimination
- communities' understanding of mental health should improve
- decreasing negative attitudes towards mental health difficulties

Six high level objectives **(HM Government UK, 2011)**

Supporting the emotional health of primary-aged children

In 2014, the National Institute for Health and Care Excellence (NICE) updated its pathway for supporting the social and emotional wellbeing of children within primary education. The aim of the pathway is to act as a framework for commissioners and service providers to help inform provision planning and delivery. It identifies three main strands of essential provision, each linked to specific national policies and best-practice recommendations:

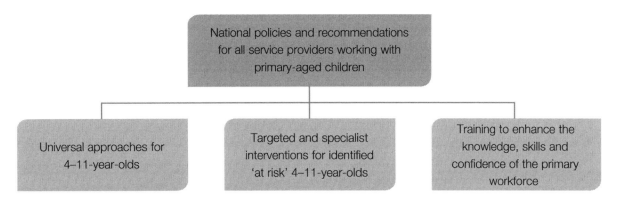

Social and emotional wellbeing in primary education (NICE, 2014)

1 Universal approaches for all 4–11-year-olds

The pathway recognises the importance of developing a series of strategies and procedures to support the emotional health and wellbeing of all primary-aged children as part of a universal approach within all primary settings, including schools. The pathway highlights four ways in which settings can develop a preventative comprehensive universal framework of supportive provision:

1 Supporting national policies and best-practice recommendations.

2 Working in partnership with relevant specialist providers in a stepped-care approach.

3 Developing a shared whole-school culture that integrates positive emotional wellbeing across all aspects of the curriculum.

4 Supporting and working in partnership with parents and families.

> **Stepped-care approach**
>
> *A model of service provision that offers a pathway of layered support. Usually this will begin with accessing the least intensive intervention appropriate to the child's needs, with the option of stepping up or down the pathway as needs change*

2 Targeted and specialist interventions for identified 'at risk' 4–11-year-olds

The pathway further recommends that vulnerable children, such as those with SEN, should be recognised early within the primary education process through a robust identification and assessment process. The children involved in this stage of the pathway may already show early signs of emotional distress, or be identified as being 'at risk' of developing emotional and/or mental health difficulties. These children should be provided with specialist and targeted interventions to help support and strengthen their emotional resilience. Additionally, practitioners working in education may offer focused support to parents of children considered 'at risk' through group-based programmes (perhaps running these jointly with colleagues in health and social care settings) and provide parents with details of the school's policies on supporting children's emotional wellbeing.

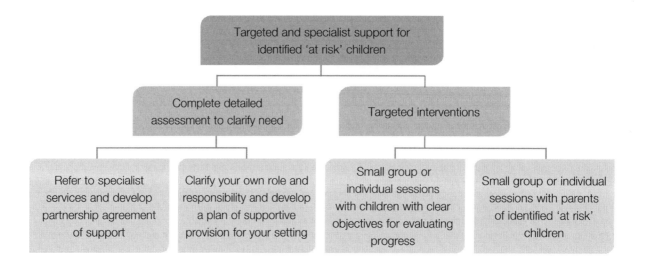

3 Training to enhance the knowledge, skills and confidence of the primary workforce

The third strand of provision recommended by NICE involves developing a pathway of training for all practitioners working within primary settings. It recognises the importance of developing the knowledge and skills of education-based practitioners in promoting and enhancing the mental health of young children, both at a universal level (i.e. whole-school approaches) and at a targeted level for identified 'at risk' children (i.e. personalised provision). This will ensure practitioners are supporting children's emotional needs appropriately and competently. Individuals need to confidently know what their role is and what their responsibilities are, and recognise when it is necessary to refer a child to specialist mental health services.

A comprehensive model of early intervention

Offering appropriate support and intervention at the earliest opportunity means a more proactive and preventative service model. The growing evidence base for effective interventions to build emotional resilience and promote better mental health in children highlights both the short-term and long-term impacts of intervening early. Statistics considering the financial impact of early intervention show that children with significant behavioural and conduct difficulties in their primary education years will go on to cost public services ten times more by the time they are adults than children without these difficulties. Positive interventions such as parenting and family support programmes, which have a proven impact upon children with persistent conduct issues, would cost the taxpayer significantly less (Scott et al., 2001).

The term 'early intervention' was primarily applied to supporting vulnerable young children (aged 0–3 years), following the recognition that offering early support to them and their families was effective in breaking the cycle of deprivation and helping these children develop stronger social, emotional and physical health. The long-term impact of this early input was that children achieved more in school, increased their chances of being productive and positive adults within their communities, and became more competent parents themselves in the future. Early intervention is now more globally recognised and utilised as an important intervention for all children and young people through various stages of childhood, and is not just considered valuable for those of pre-school age.

A model that proposes the importance of prevention and early intervention in supporting the emotional needs of primary-aged children was highlighted in the *Mental health and behaviour in schools* guidance report (DfE, 2014a). This document recognises the importance of schools providing a comprehensive range of opportunities and interventions for children to engage in, which will help build their emotional skills and enhance their emotional wellbeing.

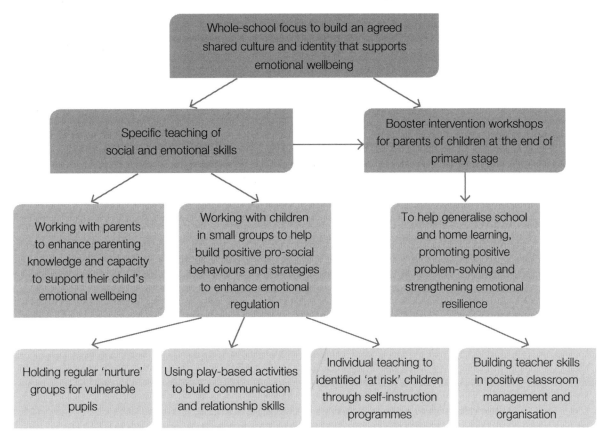

Informed by *Mental health and behaviour in schools* (DfE, 2014a)

Pro-social

Behaviour that is undertaken to benefit or help someone else

The provision of support during austere times

In today's challenging economic times, it is important to consider the impact of financial pressures upon services that support children's emotional wellbeing, especially those children with SEN. A recent report by the National Children's Bureau (NCB) (2012) looked at the impact of an estimated £405 million cut in statutory funding that 34,000 charities supporting vulnerable children and their families in England face between 2012 and 2017. The report concluded that for numerous of these charities, this difficult economic context would prove too much, with many of them indicating that it was likely they would have to close. For the families with children with SEN who rely upon these charitable services, this is likely to have a significant negative impact.

Similar concerns have been expressed by YoungMinds, the UK-based organisation that looks to highlight and support the needs of young people with emotional wellbeing and mental health issues. Their recent enquiry into the funding of Child and Adolescent Mental Health Services (CAMHS) budgets in 51 LAs in England indicated that two thirds had already reduced their funding into CAMHS, and many were expecting to have to continue reducing funding into these services over the coming years. The impact of this reduction for many communities will be significant. It is likely to result in fewer specialist mental health practitioners within localities, putting greater strain upon already stretched services. Vital specialist services offering preventative and early intervention input will be at most risk (YoungMinds, 2011).

A robust provision of emotional and mental health support would provide input across the four strands or 'tiers' of service delivery. The more complex and persistent the needs of the children, the greater the likelihood of needing support from higher up the tier system.

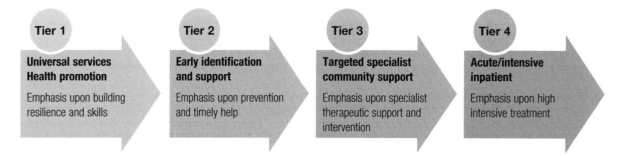

The government strategy *No health without mental health* (HM Government UK, 2011) highlights how important good mental health is for children and recognises the valuable role early intervention can play in preventing the onset of mental health difficulties both in childhood and later life, and mitigating against their impact when they occur.

> *The* No health without mental health *strategy takes a life course approach, recognising that the foundations for lifelong wellbeing are already being laid down before birth, and that there is much we can do to protect and promote wellbeing and resilience through our early years, into adulthood and then on into a healthy old age.*
>
> (HM Government UK, 2011)

Worryingly, a reduction in funding for children's mental health services and resources is likely to lead to a more reactive (rather than proactive or preventative) response from specialist services. The focus for their increasingly scarce resources will inevitably be upon high-need presenting children with significant mental health disorders, rather than supporting multi-agency interventions that look to work proactively in providing early intervention responses to 'at risk' children within a preventative framework of promoting emotional support and resilience.

The difficult financial times specifically impact children with SEN. The Children's Society report *4 in every 10* (2011) examines the increasing numbers of children with SEN who live in poverty, estimating this rising figure to be around 320,000 in England alone. The additional care responsibilities often associated with looking after a child with SEN means that many families are unable to work, or have to work fewer hours compared to families with a child without SEN. Whilst the government has held a long-term aim to eradicate child deprivation with its *2020 Children's Plan* goal (HM Government UK, 2007) – 'no child should live in poverty' – the austere economic climate continues to challenge this ambition for those with SEN. The Children's Society report highlights the impact of poverty upon children's emotional wellbeing. Children from lower-income families are significantly less likely to report feeling positive about their lives and happy in themselves than those from higher-income families. Poverty is a particular challenge for the families of children with SEN who may need additional support and resources simply to engage in everyday activities. Without these resources, children with SEN are at risk of becoming even more disadvantaged and socially isolated.

Poverty permeates every facet of children's lives from economic and material disadvantages, through social and relational constraints and exclusions, to the personal and more hidden aspects of poverty associated with shame, sadness and the fear of difference and stigma.

(Ridge, 2009)

The long-term impact of financial constraints upon the support given to children with SEN and their families through general and specialist service provision is as yet unknown. It is clear that many practitioners supporting these children are working in difficult conditions with increasing pressures and demands. Practitioners need to work creatively, innovatively and ever more effectively, often with less support and resources, to meet the needs of this complex and vulnerable group of children. It is of vital importance that everyday working practice aiming to enhance the emotional wellbeing of children with SEN is developed to meet the aspirations of the most recent key governmental policies. The challenge is to strengthen and secure the good practice that currently exists within localities whilst providing additional resources, guidance and support to further build upon this essential, life-changing provision.

Key chapter points

⚙ *The term 'special educational needs' describes a range of behaviours and difficulties that can include: physical or sensory impairments; speech or language and communication difficulties; cognitive disabilities; medical health conditions; and emotional, social and behavioural difficulties.*

⚙ *Children with SEN are a vulnerable group at high risk of developing mental health difficulties, with prevalence estimates suggesting they are six times more likely to have emotional and mental health issues than children without SEN.*

⚙ *Recent government legislation, including the Children and Families Act (2014) and the SEND Code of Practice (2015), have led to a greater recognition of the importance of social, mental health and emotional wellbeing, and the impact it can have upon a child's ability to develop and achieve.*

⚙ *Services and practitioners are increasingly being expected to meet the emotional needs of children with SEN as part of the core support they offer.*

⚙ *NICE's Social and emotional wellbeing in primary education pathway identifies how national policies and recommendations can be used to help support children through:*

  ▪ *universal provision for all*

  ▪ *targeted and specialist interventions for 'at risk' children*

  ▪ *focused training to enhance practitioners' skills and knowledge.*

⚙ *Settings and practitioners are working within particularly challenging financial times and this will undoubtedly have an impact upon how provision and services are configured and delivered. The challenge for the future is to continue to strengthen existing practice whilst building and developing new ways of working.*

CHAPTER 2
Important childhood developmental milestones and transitions

Throughout childhood, infants and young children pass through a number of key stages in their development as they learn and become accomplished in a complex range of skills and strengths across four main areas:

1 physical and sensory development

2 cognitive and language acquisition

3 emotional and social growth

4 moral and personal progression.

Whilst there are observable similarities or patterns in the abilities of many children of a similar chronological age during typical development, there can be a wide spread of actual mastery and competence of particular skills. Unfortunately, a number of different factors can negatively impact upon a child's developmental progress. These can include:

✿ genetic influences (such as inherited conditions or predispositions to particular difficulties)

✿ acquired limitations (such as from pre- and post-natal birth complications or traumatic brain injury)

✿ physical illness or disabilities (especially if chronic or severe) which limit the child's opportunity for practice and learning

✿ environmental context (including the experience of spending significant periods of time in surroundings which are under-stimulating and restricting)

✿ relationships with key carers (such as the development of a difficult attachment with a carer who is inconsistent in their responses and shows limited nurturing and warmth to a child).

Neurotypical stages of emotional and social development

Later stage Early Years Foundation (aged 3–5 years)

Children typically begin to show a preference for certain peers and will begin to play successfully with other children, rather than simply playing alongside or near them. The concept of friendship is becoming important and children can talk with increasing confidence about their own preferences, likes and dislikes. At this age, most children show developing independence, including a desire to feed and toilet unaided, and many like to help adults in everyday tasks such as tidying and cleaning. Whilst they are beginning to develop some understanding regarding their own feelings, many children at this age still struggle to express and control strong emotions (such as distress, frustration and anger). Children are typically beginning to realise other people have thoughts and feelings too, and with prompting can begin considering things from someone else's point of view. Sharing and turn-taking skills are more frequently observed and a sense of humour is often noted.

Key Stage 1 (aged 5–7 years)

Children further develop their self-control over their behaviour and feelings, and have a greater understanding and appreciation for concepts such as turn-taking, including waiting patiently for their turn. Their understanding of the world and their role within it is developing and this is demonstrated through their increasing communication skills. Many children have a sense of empathy for another person, demonstrated when showing concern for and offering comfort to a peer who is hurt. Their concept of friendship is more sophisticated and they are able to independently choose and maintain friendships over longer periods of time. At this stage of development, many children prefer to play with peers of the same gender and pretend-play is more elaborate and mature than previously.

Key Stage 2 (aged 7–11 years)

Children show good competency across a range of subtle emotional and social skills. They are increasingly adept at managing their emotions and realise some situations require them to keep their thoughts private or hide their true feelings. Close friendships with particular children are often strongly held and children have a clear understanding of subtle social rules and etiquette. Children of this age have a developing idea of themselves within a wider world and social context and many begin to show skills in ethical decision-making. As they get older, the influences of their peer group and educational context become increasingly important and they often express different attitudes and ideas from those held by their family or in their home context. Language skills are further enhanced, allowing children to effectively communicate their thoughts and emotions in more sophisticated ways, with increasing appropriateness to any changes in the setting or context.

Three key aspects of development which impact upon emotional and social wellbeing

1 Attachment

There is a large evidence base that highlights the positive relationship between young children having secure attachment(s) with key carers and demonstrating an increased emotional resilience to combat stress and adversity (Werner, 1990). This attachment bond appears to offer the child significant protection both during their early childhood and in their future lives, as it is highly correlated with the ability to form positive social relationships when they are older. Attachment bonds therefore represent a crucial aspect of early development, beginning with the care an infant receives as a baby and continuing through early childhood into the teenage years.

It has been found that the type of care which is most likely to create secure and positive attachment bonds is characterised by a parenting style which is warm and sensitive, responsive to the child's needs and temperament, containing and stimulating. An infant or young child will be encouraged to explore their world and stimulate their senses from the security of their positive attachment base. If these experiences are repeated often enough, connections between brain cells strengthen and learning occurs. Werner (1990) noted that providing children with familiar experiences and routines helps them develop an understanding of how their world works, which builds a positive mental structure in their mind. Whilst most children will develop positive attachment bonds with their parent(s), this may not be the case for all. What is crucially important is that a child has the opportunity to develop a secure attachment to a key adult in their environment, whether that be an extended family member or another adult within their support network.

Primary-aged children who have insecure early attachment relationships can benefit from developing positive secure relationships with other adults as part of a positive targeted intervention. Research shows their unhelpful internal model of relating to others can be positively modified.

Feeney & Noller, 1996

It appears that these important early relationships form a model or template for future relationships with others. Daniel & Wassell (2003) found that a child who feels loved and is encouraged to develop their skills and competencies by adults being dependable, available and nurturing feels emotionally contained and effective in their world. This builds their self-esteem and confidence and helps them feel able to cope and deal with unexpected events and form positive relationships with others.

Emotional containment

When one person (e.g. a mother) is able to receive and understand the emotions of another (e.g. a child) without feeling overwhelmed by them, helping that other person to cope with and manage their emotions effectively

However, a child who experiences less positive and supportive care may feel rejected, unloved and unprepared for the world, which appears uncertain and confusing to them. Their experience of adults as inconsistent tends to make them suspicious of others, and they often consider people to be unreliable and untrustworthy as a result. This often leads them to feel less confident in their social interactions, and means creating friendships and positively responding to the advances of others can be challenging. A child with insecure attachment may show less emotional awareness and understanding of how they are feeling and their skills in regulating their emotions may be limited.

Like all children, those with special educational needs (SEN) are able to develop secure attachments with suitable caregiving and environmental support. However, the development of these key attachment relationships may be more complex due to the additional needs of the child which influence their language and communication skills, their cognitive understanding of a situation, and their social desire and responses.

Attachment behaviours can fall within one of several patterns of response. Young children with secure attachment play happily when their main carer is present, but often become upset if they leave, and may require comfort from them when the carer returns. The child is wary of strangers and often seeks comfort and reassurance from their main carer if they are frightened or hurt.

By contrast, children with insecure attachment may avoid contact with their main carer and seem to shun them after a period of separation, appearing equally content to interact with unfamiliar adults and seek their attention and care. They may appear resistant to comfort and can be emotionally confused and uncertain in their responses.

2 Theory of mind

> **Theory of mind**
>
> *The ability to understand that other people have thoughts and feelings different to our own*

The development of theory of mind, where a child becomes more aware of and skilled in understanding what other people may be thinking or feeling, usually occurs during the first six years of life. Whilst the majority of typically-developing children will develop these skills fairly intuitively through their everyday interactions with others without any particularly focused teaching, children with SEN may struggle to acquire theory of mind without support and targeted intervention. Children with autism in particular are often felt to show some level of 'mind blindness', a term commonly used to describe a difficulty in recognising and understanding the feelings and thoughts of others. Children with delays in their general development or cognitive skills may also struggle to develop theory of mind. With support, many of these children will go on to develop these skills, albeit at a later chronological age to their typically-developing peers, or at a simpler level of understanding.

One of the first tests of a child's theory of mind was demonstrated by Wimmer & Perner (1983) in their famous Sally-Anne Test. Practitioners can use this simple play activity to help assess a child's understanding of how different characters are thinking and feeling in a situation.

The Sally–Anne Test

Sally has a basket and Anne has a box. Sally puts her marble in her basket and leaves the room. When she is gone, Anne takes the marble and puts it in her box. When Sally comes back into the room, where does she look to find her marble?

Children who have poorly-developed theory of mind will struggle to understand that Sally does not know her marble has been moved from her basket into the box. They rely upon their own knowledge without considering the experiences of the other person. Therefore, they will say Sally will look in the box, not the basket, for the marble.

Having difficulties in developing theory of mind often leads children to struggle in their emotional communications and social interactions. They may appear egocentric in their actions as they are usually driven by their own motivations and understanding of what is happening in a situation, and they can seem unresponsive or insensitive to the actions or responses of other children. A lack of theory of mind may lead to a child being unsure of how to make sense of the world around them. They may become easily confused or anxious, especially in unfamiliar settings or if routines are changed unexpectedly. They may also find it hard to predict what people might do next, or know how they are expected to behave as a situation or context changes.

3 Independence

An important part of early development for a young child is their ability to develop independence from their carers in order to become increasingly self-reliant in dealing with difficulties or problems and new experiences and settings. Childhood involves a number of key transitions, some common to most children and others specific or individual to a particular child or sibling group.

Typical transition experiences most children face include:

- developing wider social relationships and bonds with adults other than their key attachment figure, independent from this figure
- making and losing relationships, such as friendships with peers and different class teachers
- learning the skills to feed, dress and toilet independently
- moving from a familiar environment to a less familiar one with new routines and demands
- comforting and settling themselves independently when hurt or going to sleep
- having to problem-solve and make their own choices independently and without support.

Generally, parents and carers need to allow children the opportunity to develop age-appropriate autonomy whilst balancing their physical safety and emotional wellbeing at the same time. This is often more challenging to achieve for those supporting children with SEN. Some parents may feel over-protective about their child and unsure of how to help them develop their independence. Indeed, some adults may question whether independence is a realistic or appropriate goal for the child to aim for. Practitioners need to ensure they communicate regularly with parents of children with SEN regarding these issues as the child develops. Ideally, all those supporting a child with SEN will collaboratively work together to ensure they are aspirational in their expectations and desires for the child, whilst being sensitive to their actual needs and abilities and pragmatic in their ongoing skills target-setting.

Sometimes it is useful to have a key long-term goal or vision which can be broken down into a number of short-term goals or progression steps. By systematically working through the more manageable and achievable short-term goals, both the parents and child with SEN will experience tangible success. Over time, these steps will add together to build essential competencies and skills for meeting the longer-term objective.

Promoting independence in children with SEN to help them successfully cope with change and key transitional stages is an important aspect of the support and care practitioners and parents provide. By encouraging children (where appropriate) to make a choice when presented with two or more options, a parent is giving a confident and respectful message to the child about their belief in the child being able to choose for themselves. By allowing a child to physically explore an environment, to try new tasks and challenge themselves with something unfamiliar, the parent is telling the child that it is safe and good to try to learn to do something previously unknown. Similarly, when a parent positively encourages another adult to play, support or care for their child, this tells the child that other adults can also be fun to be with and can be trusted and approached for help if needed.

The impact of SEN upon emotional and social development

It is very common for children with SEN to struggle with their emotional, social and personal development. Sometimes the nature of the child's SEN, such as cognitive or sensory limitations, directly impacts upon their ability to learn and develop skills in these key areas of development. Children with profound intellectual limitations often have difficulties in comprehending and expressing language, which impacts significantly upon their ability to communicate and respond socially to others. Cognitive limitations often lead to difficulties in interpersonal problem-solving, and many children with SEN find it hard to think of suitable solutions to social problems and manage the complex emotions they may experience at these moments. Additionally, they may have physical or sensory disabilities which can create challenges to being able to respond appropriately to peers in social contexts.

For other children with SEN, the negative impact upon their emotional and social learning is more indirect and occurs as a result of experiencing fewer opportunities for observing and practising skills with an appropriate peer group. This may especially be the case for some children who attend specialist residential schools or special schools, who may have limited experience of interacting with peers without SEN or disabilities. As a result, children with SEN and disabilities are often more socially isolated and restricted in their social experiences and opportunities to take part in a wide range of appropriate activities. It is important that parents and practitioners within the child's home and school contexts consider how best to facilitate the child's emotional and social development with a peer group and build moments for focused emotional and social learning within everyday tasks.

If a child with SEN has less chance to practise their emotional and social skills in everyday life, the gap between their abilities and competencies and those of their peers may widen. Whilst it is therefore important to provide appropriate targeted emotional and social skills intervention work for identified 'at risk' children, it is also essential that non-SEN children are supported to understand their peers with SEN better and are encouraged to respond favourably to their advances and interactions. Some of the most effective interventions to build and strengthen social and emotional skills are those which include a mix of children with and without SEN.

How SEN difficulties may be observed in a child's behaviour

Presenting concern	Possible behaviours observed		Interventions that may help
Learning needs (cognitive/intellectual, global or specific)	These children may: • be easily distracted and inattentive • struggle to change or transition to another activity • prefer to play with younger children • have difficulty problem-solving • not generalise their learning from one setting to another.		• Keep language simple and direct. • Avoid sudden changes in routines or activities. • Support tasks with visual and behavioural cues to help the child understand what is expected of them. • Break down tasks into manageable steps. • Allow for practice and repetition.
Physical health needs (global or specific)	These children may: • have difficulties walking or running • have poor balance • be unable to release objects • have poorly-developed fine motor skills • struggle with writing or drawing • withdraw from activities that require physical dexterity and skill as these activities may increase their emotional response (e.g. frustration, anxiety, anger).		• Consider and make appropriate modifications to the physical environment (e.g. avoid area rugs, check doors are wide enough for frames or wheelchair access). • Differentiate lesson plans and class activities to accommodate and support physical health needs in order to maximise inclusion and active participation.
Sensory needs (global or specific)	*Hearing*	These children may: • interrupt conversations or not talk very much • struggle to follow verbal instructions • not respond when spoken to.	• Check environment and equipment is appropriate. • Provide children with more visual cues. • Cut down on background noise. • Support verbal language with gestures and facial expressions.
	Visual	These children may: • appear inattentive • complain of headaches after completing activities • avoid bright lights • often stumble or fall.	• Be sensitive to sensory environmental issues and make appropriate adaptations (e.g. avoid sudden changes of lighting). • Communicate task demands clearly. • Use pads on table corners. • Keep furniture in regular places.
Emotional and/or social needs (global or specific)	These children may: • show aggressive, hyperactive, or passive (withdrawal) behaviours across many situations • struggle to recognise and express a range of emotions • be restless and find it hard to concentrate on tasks • regress to immature behaviours when stressed • often struggle with peer relationships.		• Teach problem-solving skills for situations that are known to trigger difficult behaviours. • Avoid over-stimulation and keep tasks short and focused. • Develop routines and prepare children in advance for transitions. • Provide consistency in behaviour management with clear age-appropriate expectations.

Creating opportunities to help children with SEN learn

Children with SEN are more likely to develop new skills and engage in learning opportunities (including those linked to emotional development and wellbeing) if they are being supported in a caring environment that understands their needs and strengths. This environment, where necessary, needs to make appropriate adaptation to the task set to maximise the likelihood of a child with SEN's learning being successful. Additionally, it is important that children develop the right mindset for learning through a positive attitude towards completing tasks. This can be helped by ensuring that learning is enjoyable and interesting. Tasks to be completed should be manageable yet appropriately challenging, and adults around the child should provide a 'scaffold of support' which can be slowly removed as the child becomes more competent and skilled in a task.

Practitioners nurture learning in children with SEN through:

⚙ **Sensitivity**

Being understanding of the child's needs and abilities and being sensitive in their responses to the child.

⚙ **Stimulation**

Taking an active part in the child's learning to help maintain their interest, confidence and competency in completing a task.

⚙ **Autonomy**

Expertly knowing when to withdraw and allow the child to experiment and make choices, but also when to re-engage again to help support learning.

(Pascal & Bertram, 1997)

The process of learning

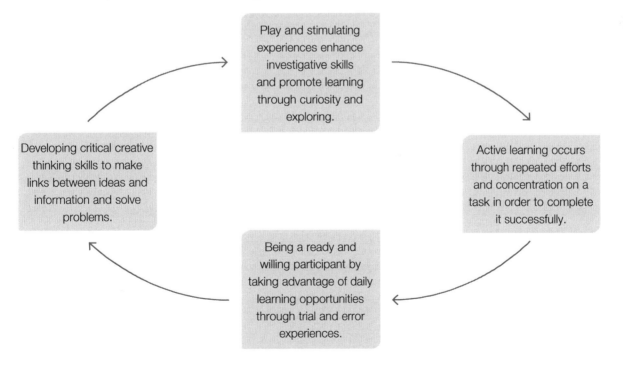

Key chapter points

⚙ *Children generally develop particular skills and abilities (often referred to as milestones) in a similar pattern and order, although there will be a spread of mastery of skills within typically-developing children.*

⚙ *Sometimes children with SEN may take longer to reach a particular milestone or may never develop an individual skill or ability without specific and targeted support and adult intervention.*

⚙ *Each child's particular pattern of development is influenced by a range of factors, including:*

- *genetic influences*
- *acquired limitations from trauma or injury*
- *physical illness or disabilities*
- *the quality of the environmental context*
- *key attachment relationships.*

⚙ *Practitioners supporting the learning of children with SEN need to be sensitive to their needs and understanding of their challenges, able to stimulate and create interest to promote curiosity and learning, and encouraging of appropriate levels of autonomy and independence for the child through knowing when to withdraw their input and when to offer active support.*

⚙ *All children (with or without SEN) are more likely to learn and develop when they feel happy and settled, interested and motivated, nurtured and supported, encouraged to be an active participant in their learning, and when teaching is appropriately personalised to consider their individual needs and strengths.*

CHAPTER 3
Mental health difficulties in primary-aged children

What defines good mental health?

Whilst there may be some individual differences between children, there are a number of common factors or characteristics that are commonly observed in primary-aged children who are felt to demonstrate and experience good emotional health.

An emotionally-resilient child:

- knows they have someone close who loves them unconditionally
- will confide their thoughts and feelings in someone when needed
- is able to play or work independently
- has a positive outlook on life
- is willing to try new things
- likes to achieve things and receive praise
- likes themselves
- has confidence in their own abilities
- has a sense of humour
- has plans and ideas
- has people they know they can count on to help them.

(Grotberg, 1997)

Important definitions

There are a number of terms that are often used interchangeably when describing the mental health of children. It is important to be clear about the distinctions between **emotional health and wellbeing**, **mental health concerns or difficulties**, and a **mental health illness or disorder**.

Emotional health and wellbeing

Emotional health refers to a child's inner experience of wellbeing as defined through their ability to be aware of how they are feeling and manage their own emotions, as well as how they are able to respond to the feelings and behaviours of others in ways that are helpful and not harmful to themselves. The term reflects the emotional state they experience, which is influenced by a range of environmental, biological, social, cognitive and behavioural factors. Their level of competency and skill in responding to their thoughts and feelings, the actions of others and the world around them will influence their state of emotional health and wellbeing. Sometimes the term 'emotional health' is interchanged with 'mental health', both referring to the balance of someone's internal emotional state of wellbeing.

> *Emotional wellbeing is 'a positive state of mind and body, feeling safe and able to cope, with a sense of connection with people, communities and the wider environment'.*
> **WHO, 2007**

Mental health concerns or difficulties

Mental health concerns or difficulties are often characterised as short-lived or transient episodes of distress or disturbance, often mild in severity and usually associated with a tangible or identifiable trigger within a child's environment or life experience (e.g. the onset of important school exams, transitioning from primary to secondary school, the birth of a sibling, peer group difficulties). Due to their short-lived nature, many mental health concerns can often be successfully influenced by targeted interventions. These can help a child overcome their difficulties and return to a state of good emotional wellbeing. These interventions can be school-based and are often informed by consultation with specialist mental health providers.

Mental health illness or disorder

Mental health illnesses or disorders are usually those diagnosed by a specialist mental health professional where a child's presenting symptoms, which are of moderate to severe intensity, are compared against an agreed set of criteria as noted in a diagnostic framework such as the International Classification of Disorders (ICD) or the Diagnostic Statistical Manual (DSM). Where appropriate, a formal diagnosis is then made and in some cases medication may be offered. Unlike children with mental health concerns or difficulties, a child with a mental health illness or disorder should be supported through specialist mental health interventions that are co-ordinated and reviewed by qualified mental health professionals. For these children, specialist therapeutic interventions are often offered and progress and input is monitored and reviewed by the qualified mental health professionals working across Tier 3 or Tier 4 of the Child and Adolescent Mental Health Services (CAMHS) if needed. These children often experience symptoms which are highly distressing, complex and persistent and may require professional mental health input over a long period of time. Much can be done within an educational setting to help support specialist mental health input, and professionals from a range of services can work together to provide a consolidated and co-ordinated layered system of support which offers greater assistance to the child and their family.

Common mental health disorders of childhood

A large-scale prevalence study of mental health disorders in children in Britain has not been completed for over a decade. The last study for the Office of National Statistics in 2004 indicated that the most common type of mental health disorders in primary-aged children were (in order):

1 Conduct or behavioural disorders

2 Anxiety disorders

3 Disorders of attention and hyperactivity

4 Depression

5 Eating disorders.

Historically, boys have been more likely to develop a mental health difficulty than girls. The large surveys of mental health in children and adolescents across the UK have previously found that around 10% of boys and 5% of girls aged between five and ten years had mental health concerns.

Current estimates of prevalence support a similar slight gender imbalance until the teenage years, when the gender gap lessens but actual prevalence increases to 13% of boys and 10% of girls experiencing mental health problems.

Murphy & Fonagy, 2012

Conduct or behavioural disorders

Generally, this term is used to describe a group of behaviours that occur persistently over a given time and include:

- ⚙ defiance and disobedience (e.g. episodes of lying, argumentative and manipulative behaviours)

- ⚙ a challenging and negative attitude towards authority (e.g. showing oppositional behaviours, refusing to engage)

- ⚙ routine displays of emotional volatility (e.g. having anger outbursts, having poor control over temper and emotions)

- ⚙ aggressive acts towards other people or animals.

Additionally, occurrences of anti-social behaviour (e.g. property destruction, theft and serious rule violation such as running away) can also be seen.

Children with conduct disorders are also increasingly likely to suffer with attention difficulties, impulsivity and hyperactivity, and emotional disorders. At primary school age, boys are much more likely than girls to experience significant disorders of conduct, although interestingly, once adolescence begins the prevalence of these difficulties in girls increases significantly. Most successful interventions to reduce conduct difficulties often involve the child and their parent(s) and wider family members working together.

Emotional disorders

This term describes a broad range of difficulties that impact upon emotional wellbeing and are characterised by feelings of distress, low mood and/or anxieties

> Many children with conduct difficulties are unpopular with their peers, have low self-esteem, struggle to express their emotions appropriately and have a limited understanding of social rules. A significant number also have specific learning needs.
>
> School-based interventions that may help include:
>
> - proactive positive classroom management strategies (e.g. use of praise and positive reinforcement, giving of responsibilities)
>
> - small-group teaching looking at building social competence and problem-solving skills
>
> - targeted support for learning needs.

Anxiety disorders

A commonly-seen disorder in many children involves significant and recurring anxious feelings and behaviours. The term 'anxiety disorder' is an umbrella term that includes a range of symptoms which may manifest themselves in different ways in different children. It can include signs of:

- ✿ a marked fear or phobia
- ✿ panic attacks
- ✿ social or school-related phobias
- ✿ separation anxieties
- ✿ obsessive/compulsive behaviours
- ✿ a generalised raised state of anxiety across most or all settings.

Primary-aged children often tend to display separation anxieties when separated from their key carer, as well as school-related phobias (often linked to attendance and social interactions). Observable symptoms are determined individually but will often include:

- ✿ distress and heightened or marked emotion when facing anxiety-provoking situations
- ✿ behavioural avoidance or marked agitation in particular settings
- ✿ physical symptoms of sweating, shaking, elevated heart rate and breathing
- ✿ patterns of negative cognitive thinking (such as expressions of self-doubt, concern over the wellbeing and safety of themselves or others, and repeated requests to leave a situation).

> Many children with anxiety issues suffer with low self-esteem, are socially isolated, struggle to manage their emotions (particularly in social situations) and have difficulty making decisions.
>
> Interventions that target anxieties linked to school-based activities (such as sitting tests or speaking in assembly) will look to develop positive strategies to manage these concerns through regular pastoral support. The most successful strategies will look at building emotional, cognitive and behavioural control.

Disorders of attention and hyperactivity

Children who are given a diagnosis of Attention Deficit Hyperactivity Disorder (ADHD) or similar (e.g. Hyperkinetic Disorder or Attention Deficit Disorder (ADD)) have difficulties which are usually characterised by:

⚙ reduced levels of concentration and attention

⚙ an inability to control responses, leading to impulsivity

⚙ a high level of over-activity or restlessness.

These difficulties tend to be observable across all settings, although there may be a relationship between the severity and frequency of the symptoms seen and the level of formal structure and effective management strategies in place. Usually there is a gender imbalance, with boys more likely to experience attention and hyperactivity difficulties than girls, as well as a high co-morbidity with other disorders (such as emotional or conduct difficulties). Some research has suggested that many children with attention difficulties also experience significant language and communication needs. Love & Thompson (1988) found that as many as 50% of children with ADD also had notable speech and language impairments. Other research, such as that of Richter (1995), has highlighted a strong correlation between the presence of ADHD and specific learning difficulties in children. These studies highlight the often complex needs of this group of children which will impact upon many aspects of their development and wellbeing.

Many children with attention and hyperactivity issues have difficulty following instructions and completing tasks, are easily distracted and appear forgetful, often interrupt others when they are speaking, and find it difficult to wait and take turns.

School-based interventions that may help include:

- setting short, focused tasks with immediate feedback and reward

- using checklists to tick off completed tasks

- keeping class rules clear and simple.

Depression

Children who are diagnosed with clinical depression experience a significant low mood which is persistent and severe in intensity over a period of time. Other symptoms include:

⚙ an increase in irritability

⚙ withdrawal from activities the child used to enjoy

⚙ difficulties concentrating or being interested in learning

⚙ expressions of marked distress and self-harm.

Additionally, a child with depression may also present with physical signs of ill health, such as stomach pains and headaches, difficulty sleeping and loss of appetite. Depression can impact upon all aspects of a child's life, including their relationships with peers and family members. Most children with clinically-diagnosed depression will receive support from specialist mental health practitioners. However, schools have a valuable role to play in supporting any interventions suggested and continuing to build positive school-based experiences for the child in order to strengthen their emotional wellbeing.

Many children develop depression following a significant incident or life event, such as family breakdown, bullying or loss of a loved one. They may show a loss of confidence and decline in academic performance or skills, or experience fatigue and express thoughts of being useless or inadequate.

School-based interventions that may help include:

- working on any underlying school problem that can be solved and managed through regular and effective pastoral support systems

- building positive social opportunities to help regain social confidence and interpersonal skills.

Eating disorders

Eating disorders are less prevalent in primary-aged children than other mental health disorders, but are nonetheless highly distressing and challenging to manage when present. Symptoms can include a range of cognitive, emotional and behavioural difficulties, including a distortion of body image, physical changes (e.g. in body weight), and a low or anxious mood. Children with eating disorders require specialist mental health as well as general medical health support, which often involves professionals from a range of services and agencies. Schools should be guided by these professionals regarding how they can support the child in the most appropriate and effective manner and further consolidate and strengthen the specialist interventions already being delivered. An eating disorder will likely have a negative impact upon the self-esteem of the child, their confidence and ability to take part in positive social interactions with their peers, and their learning and academic achievements.

Children who develop eating disorders often withdraw from social relationships and experience emotional distress, particularly around mealtimes which they find difficult to manage.

School-based interventions that may help include:

- developing opportunities to help build self-esteem and confidence

- encouraging positive social experiences through facilitated (adult-supported) activities within their peer groups.

Somatisation

Somatisation

The genuine experience of physiological pain and bodily complaints which have an undetermined physical origin and are more likely to be attributed to a psychological or emotional cause

Primary-aged children often express their psychological distress through complaints regarding bodily wellbeing and functioning. Characteristically, these physical complaints are usually genuinely experienced by the child but do not solely have an organic origin (such as infection or tissue damage), and psychological factors often play a more significant role in the symptoms' development and maintenance. It is helpful to consider children's somatic symptoms as occurring somewhere on a dimension which has actual physiological or bodily factors at one end and psychological influences at the other. It is often very difficult to establish how much of a role psychological factors have in impacting upon a child's experience of genuine pain and ill health.

Research suggests that somatic difficulties can be seen as part of a broader dimension of internalising behavioural problems (Achenbach, 1991). It is commonly found that children whose general cognitive functioning is between the ages of two and four years are more likely to:

⚙ experience somatic elimination complaints (such as suffering with regular constipation or diarrhoea or showing resistance to using the toilet)

⚙ demonstrate a reduced appetite (including food refusal)

⚙ commonly engage in breath-holding.

In contrast, children whose general cognitive functioning is between the ages of five and 11 years are more likely to show somatic health concerns linked to:

⚙ stomach problems (including pains, nausea and vomiting)

⚙ headaches (often with associated eye problems and tiredness)

⚙ skin problems (often linked with soreness and painful movement).

This is useful to remember when considering the needs of children with SEN who may have significant cognitive difficulties and as such may be functioning at a lower emotional, social or cognitive level than their actual chronological age.

Achenbach (1991) also found that children who are vulnerable to developing somatic complaints can benefit from helpful interventions centred on building skills in effective emotional expression, self-empowerment and locus of control. Additionally, many of these children experience underlying anxiety and can therefore be supported through developing more effective stress and anxiety management strategies, including relaxation exercises. Building a child's emotional resilience will help buffer them against everyday life stresses and should provide them with a greater sense of control and confidence. In turn, somatic complaints should diminish over time.

> **Locus of control**
>
> *The extent to which someone feels they can control or influence what happens to them. Someone with a strong internal locus of control believes they play a significant role in influencing events and their outcomes*

Emotional and mental health difficulties in children with SEN

When working with children with complex learning needs, it is sometimes a challenge for practitioners to distinguish the behaviours and difficulties that arise from the child's cognitive needs from those that arise as a result of a mental health disorder.

Coughlan (2010) found that many school-based practitioners working with children with complex SEN report a lack of clarity over what constitutes a mental health disorder and confusion over how to identify these concerns within this group of vulnerable pupils. They noted that sometimes it is assumed that mental health difficulties are simply part of the child's condition (such as marked

'Very often, mental health difficulties present in atypical or unusual ways in people with an intellectual disability, and so often go unrecognised for significant periods of time'.
Coughlan, 2010

anxieties and obsessive behaviours in children with autism) and this can impact upon people's expectations of how a child can progress and which behaviours can change.

When responding to these dilemmas, it is highly important that if concerns are raised about the mental health and emotional wellbeing of a child with SEN, then the adults who know that child well must be actively involved in any assessment process completed by a specialist mental health practitioner. These adults will play a key role in helping the practitioner understand the child better through providing an insight into key aspects of the child's behaviour, wellbeing and development, including:

- ✿ the child's areas of strength, interests and activities that bring them pleasure
- ✿ the child's areas of challenge and difficulty across all aspects of functioning and development
- ✿ the child's usual temperament and personality, learning and coping style preferences
- ✿ any noticeable changes observed in the child's responses, behaviours or development in recent weeks or months
- ✿ any important information regarding the family, social or educational setting that will help inform the assessment.

Specialist practitioners may need to undertake a prolonged assessment to fully explore the emotional needs of the child, which will likely include observations of the child in different settings and discussions with key adults in the child's life. It may also include a formal assessment of strengths and weaknesses in order to build an accurate profile of the child's level of functioning and potential. As with all children, it is important that an individual, personalised approach is taken during the assessment in order to understand key issues, such as how a child with SEN may communicate (i.e. through words, actions and/or behavioural responses) and how they make sense of their world. Specialist mental health practitioners with experience and knowledge of SEN will be better placed to understand the complex presentation of children with SEN and mental health concerns. These skills will help guide a practitioner in making a more accurate distinction between difficulties and concerns linked to a child's learning needs from those linked to a child's mental health needs.

Risk and protective factors

There is a complex relationship between the presence of mental health difficulties in children and the interplay of psycho-biological-social factors evident within their wider family and environmental context. This relationship has led to a greater understanding of the role of risk and protective factors in influencing a child's emotional wellbeing. Research suggests that children are more likely to develop mental health difficulties if:

- ✿ they live in a single-parent household rather than a two-parent household
- ✿ they live in a community with high deprivation rather than living in a more affluent community
- ✿ a parent suffers with mental health difficulties
- ✿ they live with parents who have few academic qualifications rather than those with a degree-level education

✿ they witness domestic violence

✿ they have a physical health illness (compared with those children with good physical health).

(Davies, 2012)

Risk factors

Risk factors are defined as observable factors within a child, their family, and their wider context which are known to increase the likelihood of the child developing a mental health difficulty. Calculating this risk is a complex process as it is highly dependent upon the relationships between individual factors. However, the evidence base for determining risk factors is well-established and provides a coherent picture regarding factors which impact upon emotional health and how these can influence the likelihood of a child becoming mentally unwell.

Known risk factors

Risk factors within the child	• low self-esteem and self-worth • physical illness (including long-term chronic pain) • genetic predisposition to mental health issues • specific and global learning difficulties • communication difficulties • problems with social relationships • a 'difficult' personality or temperament
Risk factors within the family	• family breakdowns (including parental separation) • parental mental health problems • limited parenting capacity, especially in relation to the child's changing emotional, cognitive and general developmental needs • death or loss of key family members • parental involvement in criminality, drug or alcohol abuse, or domestic violence • difficult family relationships, particularly between parent and child
Risk factors within the wider community context	• being part of a community or educational setting with low aspirations • living in a community that is socially and economically disadvantaged • experiencing homelessness and poverty • living with intolerance, prejudice and discrimination • attending a school that experiences unpredictable change

It is generally acknowledged that there is a cumulative effect in that the greater number of risk factors a child experiences, the greater the probability that the child may go on to experience mental health difficulties. The Department for Education and Skills document *Promoting children's mental health within early years and school settings* (DfES, 2001) suggests a child who has one identified risk factor has a probability of around 1–2% of developing a mental health difficulty. That figure increases to 8% if they experience three risk factors, and significantly increases to 20% if four or more risk factors are evident.

Protective factors

There are also known qualities which can exist within a child, their family, and their wider context which are known to buffer or protect a child against the likelihood of developing a mental health problem. These protective factors, often referred to as factors which increase the emotional resilience of a child, are vitally important when considering how to improve and strengthen a child's emotional wellbeing. Research, including that of Werner & Smith (1992), is consistent regarding the nature of many of these protective factors, and therefore settings and parents can be confident in building upon these when looking to promote and strengthen a child's mental health and emotional wellbeing. To a certain extent, one can counterbalance against some of the risk factors that may be impacting on a child by building upon known protective factors.

Known protective factors

Protective factors within the child	• experience of secure and nurturing early attachments • an 'easy' temperament as an infant • an uneventful birth and good physical health as an infant and young child • effective communication and social skills • normal-range intelligence • a sense of humour • an ability to plan and problem-solve • an ability to transfer learning from one context to another
Protective factors within the family	• at least one positive parent–child attachment relationship • discipline and boundaries are clear and consistently applied within the home • the child's learning and achievements are supported and celebrated • affectionate and nurturing family relationships • positive communication demonstrated within the family • parents are supportive of the child working towards independence and successfully achieving milestones
Protective factors within the wider community context	• good-quality, secure housing • family have extended community social support • a range of social and leisure activities are available for the child to participate in • school has positive policies for enhancing emotional wellbeing • school has clear and consistently-applied procedures for managing difficult behaviour and incidents of bullying

Rutter notes that children who have good emotional resilience are more likely to have increased protection against any risk and stress factors evident in their life. He characterises resilient strengths within three areas:

1 A good sense of identity, self-esteem and confidence.
2 A firm belief in one's own self-efficacy and ability to influence, manage and control situations.
3 A wide range of effective social problem-solving skills.

(Rutter, 1985)

It may be useful to consider these three areas when looking to develop universal strategies to help promote children's emotional wellbeing and build learning opportunities for developing related skills in each area.

Risk and protective factors in children with SEN

In addition to the positive protective factors already highlighted, some studies have identified particular qualities that appear to add further protection for children with SEN from the impact of key known risk factors. Large research studies, such as that by Anders et al. (2010), provide an interesting insight into the role these factors may play in increasing the likelihood of a child with SEN reaching their potential in development and wellbeing. Further protective factors for children with SEN include:

- early identification of their levels of need
- early implementation of effective strategies to help support the child
- high-quality educational settings, especially in the early years of development
- support from knowledgeable, experienced teachers
- an educational setting which has high aspirations for the child
- emphasis upon promoting skills to help the child adjust to school and increase their readiness for learning
- a rich home learning environment
- child has some cognitive strengths and is able to communicate their needs effectively
- family home has good socio-economic status
- child had normal birth weight and does not experience ongoing physical health issues which necessitate long periods of time in hospital (thus the child being removed from their familiar supportive environment for lengthy periods of time)
- child born early in the academic year (i.e. not a summer birth)
- child born into a family of small or average size.

How can we encourage children to help themselves?

Everyone can improve their emotional wellbeing. Practitioners can support children in developing their emotional robustness through embracing certain activities and practising certain behaviours. The Mental Health Foundation has developed a list of statements that children can adopt to help build their emotional health:

Informed by *How can we help ourselves?* (Mental Health Foundation, 2015)

Key chapter points

⚙ *Emotional health is defined as our inner experience of wellbeing. It is informed by our thoughts and feelings about something, how we manage these emotions, and how effective we are in responding to the feelings and behaviours of other people.*

⚙ *Mental health concerns occur when our emotional health is compromised and we begin to experience distress, as shown through a change in our thoughts, feelings and actions.*

⚙ *Mental health disorders are persistent and diagnosable conditions, necessitating input from specialist mental health practitioners.*

⚙ *There are a number of mental health disorders commonly seen in primary-aged children. These include:*

■ *conduct or behavioural disorders*

■ *anxiety disorders*

■ *disorders of attention and hyperactivity*

■ *depression*

■ *eating disorders.*

⚙ *Sometimes it can be difficult to accurately recognise and diagnose a mental health concern in a child with SEN. Any specialist mental health assessment should involve discussions with key adults in the child's life who know them well and can help inform a better understanding of the child's difficulties and presenting needs.*

⚙ *Risk factors are identified characteristics found within a child, their family or context which are known to increase the child's likelihood of developing a mental health difficulty.*

⚙ *Protective factors are identified characteristics found within a child, their family or context which are known to help buffer against life's stresses and strains (and risk factors for that child), and help protect the child against developing a mental health difficulty.*

⚙ *It is important to recognise good emotional health and encourage and enhance positive emotional behaviours in children with SEN when they are observed.*

CHAPTER 4
Strengthening everyday practice to enhance emotional wellbeing

Developing a comprehensive framework of emotional support

The most effective provision for strengthening emotional wellbeing involves offering layers of support which are accessed according to a child's level of need. In this way, provision is readily available to support all children, with a range of effective interventions actioned to meet individual characteristics and requirements.

Universal provision for all

e.g. 'quality first' or high-quality teaching of social, emotional and behavioural skills, and effective whole-school policies and procedures for the promotion of emotional wellbeing

Small group interventions for identified children

e.g. discrete teaching to small groups regarding targeted topics and skills

Individual intervention for vulnerable children

e.g. personalised support and teaching of skills based upon identified need

Universal provision for all: whole-school approaches

Children tend to flourish emotionally in schools which have an explicit focus on supporting emotional health and wellbeing. Whole-school initiatives can create an organisational culture and environment which values children's emotional and mental health, demonstrated through the development of their social, emotional and behavioural skills. The more effective the universal provision for all children, the fewer children will require more individual or additional support.

However, children with special educational needs (SEN) are more likely to need additional support to develop their emotional health than that offered through universal strategies. This is primarily due to difficulties in accessing generic teaching without focused support or adjustment as a result of their SEN, particularly if they are complex and impact upon key areas of functioning.

The *Promoting children's mental health within early years and school settings* report (DfES, 2001) highlighted some of the qualities observed in schools that were effective in developing a whole-school approach to promoting emotional wellbeing:

- Senior management demonstrated a clear commitment to the principles and understanding of the whole-school approach.
- The school had systems in place which made sure that all individuals felt valued and listened to.
- There were observable positive adult–child, child–child and adult–adult relationships modelled in the school.
- Staff showed knowledge, confidence and skills in promoting emotional factors within a learning context.
- There were clear and consistently-implemented policies on behaviour, bullying, race equality and inclusion.
- Professional standards (including attitudes, knowledge, values, ethical decision-making and skills competencies) were observably high.
- Teaching was skilful and motivating for pupils.
- The school worked proactively with parents.
- The children were actively involved in the development and progression of their personal, social, health and economic (PSHE) learning.

Usefully, a tool was developed by the Department for Education and Skills to help audit the extent to which a school supports the emotional health of its pupils in general, called the *School self-evaluation: behaviour and attendance primary electronic audit* (DfES, 2005b). One of its tasks is to determine the extent to which a school has a whole-school ethos which promotes emotional wellbeing. It involves pupils, parents and adults who know the school well (such as grandparents, school governors, social workers and educational psychologists) who are invited to contribute to the audit evaluation. In particular, the audit examines six areas of school functioning in detail:

1 leadership and management
2 whole-school ethos
3 whole-school organisation
4 classroom practice
5 student support
6 staff development.

The tool could therefore provide a useful framework to evaluate a school's strengths and areas of need, particularly in reference to enhancing student emotional wellbeing.

See Appendix A for another framework that could be used to evaluate a school's strengths and needs.

Small group interventions for identified children: additional support

Focused interventions with small groups of children who display emotional and behavioural difficulties, and those already identified as 'at risk' of developing emotional difficulties, represent an important part of primary school mental health provision. Bailey developed a checklist of general factors which help enhance emotional wellbeing in children with SEN, which focuses upon five key areas:

1 Promoting the child behind the disability.

2 Creating a caring community.

3 Helping the child to live a fulfilled life.

4 Facilitating good physical health.

5 Supporting development and progression.

(Bailey, 2012)

This checklist could be used to help practitioners and settings consider their current provision and support offered to vulnerable children, as well as help identify areas of risk and need for further development and intervention (see Appendix B for further information).

Additionally, schools could develop a framework for their provision centred around nine characteristics commonly seen in primary settings and found to be most effective in supporting vulnerable children. These characteristics were identified in the report *Improving the attainment of looked-after children in primary schools – guidance for schools* (DfCSF, 2009).

1 Enhancing universal emotional wellbeing provision.

2 Making it a priority to know each child.

3 Linking each child to a key person.

4 Strong partnerships and relationships with relevant external people.

5 Initiating and delivering targets.

6 Ensuring consistency while adapting to changing need.

7 Balancing high levels of support with real challenge for learning.

8 Actively extending expectations for each child.

9 Planning for future transitions.

Whilst this report looked at the qualities in schools that were the most successful in enhancing the achievements and emotional wellbeing of children who were part of the looked-after system, there are similarities between this group of vulnerable children and those with SEN. For example, both are found to be at significantly increased risk of developing emotional and mental health difficulties and often find school life challenging, developing relationships difficult, and struggle to navigate through typical school transitions. It could be proposed that schools use the nine characteristics rather like a checklist to self-audit their provision and ensure a robust and comprehensive level of emotional support is offered.

Individual interventions for vulnerable children: personalised support

The level of need and abilities of a child with SEN will help inform the type of intervention and support that is required to enhance their emotional wellbeing. More able children with SEN, such as those in mainstream schools or those with a mild to moderate learning disability, are likely to respond positively to interventions that use social learning principles to teach new skills and provide opportunities within a setting to practise these. Interventions involving instruction and discussion, role-playing and practising social skills with feedback from peers or a practitioner will help a child build their emotional and social competency and confidence.

It is key that practitioners consider how these new skills can be encouraged across different contexts in order to generalise and consolidate the child's learning from their focused sessions. For example, a child may receive individual support to help them develop more effective ways of managing their feelings and communicating how they are feeling. The child can be encouraged to use these strategies when taking part in small-group work with their peers which they may often find challenging to engage in. Facilitated adult support and prompting during this small-group work can help the child successfully cope with this experience. Furthermore, these strategies can be shared with the child's wider teaching and support team to help encourage and consolidate the use of the strategies across other settings within school. This will help cement the strategies within the child's repertoire of skills and increase the likelihood of them independently initiating the use of them when the need arises.

For less able children with SEN, such as those with more profound or complex needs, different learning techniques that rely more upon the gradual shaping of new behaviours through contingency training methods may need to be introduced. The importance of providing tangible reinforcement and rewards for desired behaviours in the child often proves effective in increasing the likelihood of the new targeted behaviours occurring. Sessions will need to be frequent and short in duration, and the learning of new skills should be seen as an ongoing daily process over a number of months or even years.

Heaven (2008) argued that individual or small-group intervention programmes that look to build emotional resilience should ideally include activities that look at these specific or key components:

- ✿ promoting self-awareness
- ✿ managing feelings
- ✿ developing a positive attitude
- ✿ facilitating empathy
- ✿ building social skills.

See the *Activities to promote emotional resilience* chapter for example activities that focus on building each of these key skills.

The impact of SEN upon PSHE teaching

The principles which apply to delivering a high-quality whole-school primary curriculum which looks to build emotional and social development are relevant to all children, irrespective of their age and ability. A key way in which emotional learning is facilitated in most schools is through PSHE education. Ensuring effective and inclusive PSHE provision enables pupils with SEN to access the broader curriculum and develop valuable knowledge and skills for use in later life. However, children with disabilities and specific or complex learning needs are likely to require more personalised teaching which is sensitive to their particular strengths and needs. Expectations from teachers and adults supporting a child should be appropriate to the child's potential and considerate of how individual challenges may impact upon their learning. Modifying and adapting resources to minimise the impact of these difficulties will ensure that the emotional and social development of children with SEN is supported. Practitioners will ideally 'scaffold' or support pupils by building layers of appropriate support which can be carefully removed as the child becomes more skilled or independent, or further strengthened if the child's needs increase. Using this 'scaffolding' technique to help support and promote learning in children with SEN successfully provides a learning platform for children to develop and practise particular skills.

Wherever possible, the curriculum and programmes of study for both statutory and non-statutory subjects within primary settings should be available to all pupils. The statutory inclusion statement in the National Curriculum (DfE, 2014c) describes a framework for adapting the curriculum to meet individual pupils' needs, including those with SEN. It highlights that teachers should set all pupils learning challenges that are suitable to their particular needs and look to overcome any barriers to their learning through flexibly developing resources and modifying the curriculum where necessary, ensuring all pupils are working towards the same objective or target. To ensure inclusivity, preparation for social and emotional teaching must include prior consideration of the particular needs of individual pupils with SEN. This includes anticipation of what barriers to taking part the child might experience and consideration of how resources should be modified or adjusted to ensure all pupils have the opportunity to learn and develop. This may mean developing a parallel activity for small groups or individual pupils with SEN to run alongside the activity for the rest of the class, ensuring that all pupils are working towards the same objectives but with different processes and different levels of support and assistance.

Learning and progress assessment in PSHE may need to be flexible for pupils with SEN in order to ensure that pupils are able to demonstrate what they know and are able to do. There is a clear role for formative assessments when supporting children with SEN, which allows time for joint reflection between the child and practitioner(s) (and parents if appropriate) on progress made and discussions regarding expectations of how the child can develop further. Some pupils with SEN may not be working at Level 1 or above in the National Curriculum, and so performance descriptors (P Scales) are used to help describe a child's level of ability and attainment. These range from very early levels of learning (P Scales 1–3) through to more advanced attainment (P Scale 8), and can help document emotional and social development and identify appropriate targets for further intervention and support.

Adapting resources for use with pupils with SEN

There are a number of resources available which look at building and developing the emotional skills of primary-aged children, but few are specifically designed for children with SEN. Consequently, practitioners often need to consider if and how a resource can be adapted or modified in order for a child with SEN to gain value from it.

Ten top tips to consider when adapting programmes or activities for children with SEN

1 Remember to emphasise a child's areas of strength and ability when completing activities. This will help build confidence and increase the likelihood of their learning experience being successful.

2 Consider how you will use techniques such as role modelling, chaining tasks and providing opportunities for repeated practice when looking to teach new behaviours.

3 Look at the language used in the resource. Is it at an appropriate level for the child to understand? Can more appropriate or relevant language be used? Consider the communication supports and strategies the child currently needs and how these can be utilised to help get the most out of the resource.

4 Does the environment or setting need to be modified to help facilitate the child's learning? Consider the roles other people can play, including those outside of the school setting (such as key family members), in building upon any new skills introduced in school to help strengthen learning and transferability across settings.

5 Do modifications need to be made to any physical task needed to complete the proposed activities? Consider the child's gross and fine motor skills and whether they currently need physical support aids to facilitate their learning.

6 Consider the learning style of the child and how their skills and strengths impact upon this. Do they learn better when things are presented to them visually, orally, through tactile experience, or a combination of all senses? Try and provide new information in the style(s) which best meets their needs and consolidate the child's learning through repeated practice using a range of visual, auditory and kinaesthetic cues to help strengthen its impact.

7 Build in frequent positive progress and feedback points within a task and regularly check on the child's understanding of the activity.

8 Remember to provide praise and encouragement which explains what the child has done well and how they have improved or developed.

9 Adapt tasks by breaking them down into small, manageable chunks, keeping steps short, concise and unambiguous.

10 If appropriate, try to develop co-operation and learning amongst children by sharing tasks and responsibilities within a small group of pupils who are helped to work together towards a shared goal or outcome.

Role modelling

An effective training method to help illustrate a desirable way to behave or respond within a given situation

Chaining tasks

Breaking down tasks into individual steps which are separately mastered and then linked together to help a child complete the task as a whole

The importance of PSHE

In primary settings, PSHE is often combined with citizenship teaching as part of an important non-statutory framework of learning to help pupils become confident, healthy and happy individuals. Key Stage 1 PSHE teaching encourages children to become more aware of themselves, reflecting upon their strengths and areas of difficulty and their own position within their family, school and community. It looks to develop essential personal, social and emotional skills to help a child progress developmentally and academically and build upon knowledge and skills learnt through other subjects in the wider curriculum.

Key Stage 2 PSHE teaching further supports a child's self-reflection as they grow and change and become more mature and independent learners. Major transitions towards the end of this key stage are explored, and the skills and knowledge needed for a successful transfer into secondary education (and beyond) form an important part of this teaching.

In 2014, the PSHE Association developed ten evidence-based principles that highlight effective practice in PSHE education in primary settings:

1 Start where children are; find out what they already know, understand, are able to do and are able to say; involve them in the planning of your PSHE education programme.

2 Plan a 'spiral programme' which introduces new and more challenging learning while building on what has gone before, reflecting upon the personal developmental needs of the children.

3 Take a positive approach which focuses on what children can do to keep themselves and others healthy and safe and to lead happy and fulfilling lives.

4 Offer a wide variety of teaching and learning styles within PSHE education, with an emphasis on interactive learning with the teacher as facilitator.

5 Provide information which is realistic and relevant and which reinforces positive social norms.

6 Encourage young people to reflect on their learning and the progress they have made, and to transfer what they have learnt to say and to do from one school subject to another, and from school to their lives in the wider community.

7 Recognise that the PSHE education programme is just one part of what a school can do to help a child to develop the knowledge, skills, attitudes and understanding they need to fulfil their potential.

8 Embed PSHE education within other areas of school life to ensure children experience positive relationships with adults and feel valued, and that children identified as vulnerable are effectively supported.

9 Provide opportunities for children to make real decisions about their lives and to take part in activities which simulate adult choices, where they can demonstrate their ability to take responsibility for their decisions.

10 Provide a safe and supportive learning environment where children can develop the confidence to ask questions, challenge the information they are offered, draw on their own experiences, express their views and opinions and put what they have learnt into practice in their own lives.

In 2013, the Office for Standards in Education, Children's Services and Skills (Ofsted) reviewed the impact of PSHE teaching through evidence from their inspections in primary and secondary schools and though an online survey of young people. Their report indicates that many primary schools could improve their overall PSHE teaching by:

⚙ providing a more co-ordinated and cohesive structure of discrete PSHE learning across the year groups

⚙ ensuring that teachers are given the training and resources to teach these topics with confidence

⚙ ensuring that teachers have a comprehensive system to assess pupils' PSHE learning and progression.

Key chapter points

⚙ *A comprehensive overview of emotional support for primary settings involves three tiers:*
  1 *Effective universal provision for all pupils.*
  2 *Small group interventions for children identified as 'at risk' of emotional distress.*
  3 *Individual interventions offered to vulnerable children suffering from emotional and mental health difficulties.*

⚙ *A best-practice model for schools to effectively support the emotional wellbeing of its pupils with SEN is proposed, informed by the report on qualities found within the most effective schools supporting children within the looked-after system.*

⚙ *The most effective models involve developing a comprehensive PSHE curriculum informed by best-practice recommendations, resources and current government regulations.*

⚙ *The most beneficial provision teaches emotional wellbeing in a co-ordinated and integrated way across all year groups and enhances the school's general culture of promoting and supporting emotional health in its pupils.*

⚙ *The PSHE curriculum allows all children, including those with SEN, to build their emotional resilience and skills through targeted teaching. Resources may need to be adapted to ensure teaching is inclusive of all pupils.*

Scared

CHAPTER 5
Assessing emotional need and building emotional resilience

Assessing emotional need using a reflective-scientist practitioner model of practice

Contemporary practice requires individuals to deliver support and interventions through a structured methodology that is systematic, rigorous and transparent in its stages and process of communication. A model or framework that helps support such contemporary practice is the scientist practitioner model. This model originated in the field of clinical psychology in the late 1940s and early 1950s. Today, it is often referred to as the reflective-scientist practitioner model and is more widely used within other disciplines, including education and social care. It helps guarantee that a practitioner's work is informed by a sound evidence base and is flexible and responsive to each child's individual requirements (Baker et al., 2000).

Working as reflective-scientist practitioners to help enhance the emotional wellbeing of children with SEN allows individuals to embrace a model of daily practice which holds at its core a set of key principles:

⚙ A commitment to consider, and apply where appropriate, key literature and research knowledge to help develop a coherent theoretical understanding regarding children's development and presentation and emotional health and wellbeing.

⚙ Regular self-reflection upon activities undertaken, so demonstrating a practice that is robust, clear and accountable.

⚙ Ensuring everyday practice is dynamic and responsive to a child's individual needs and centred around their wellbeing.

⚙ Lifelong learning through a commitment to further developing practitioners' own knowledge, skills and experiences.

⚙ The sharing of experiences and learning with other practitioners in order to help build each other's professional knowledge and skills, which in turn helps contribute to further developing the evidence base.

Supporting children using a reflective-scientist practitioner framework involves undertaking a cycle (or multiple cycles) of involvement with distinct stages characterised by key activities. This way of working ensures that the most appropriate support and intervention is offered to a child and will therefore help increase the likelihood of the input being successful in making a positive difference.

Applying the reflective-scientist practitioner model to support emotional need

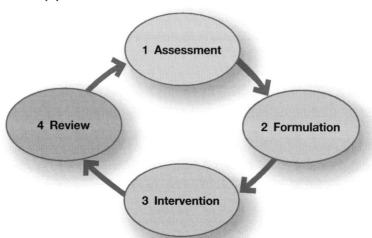

1 The cycle of involvement begins with a period of **assessment** which aims to provide a better understanding of a child's level of presenting need. This may include formal measures (tests developed with sound reliability and validity to assess functioning) and a baseline assessment of current functioning.

2 Once an initial assessment has been completed, a short period of reflection occurs which involves the development of a **formulation**. This process allows a practitioner to begin to make sense of what they have learnt about the child as well as highlight what they may still need to find out.

3 A focused **intervention** may be developed from the formulation, which should include:

- clarity over the roles and responsibilities of the people involved in delivering the intervention
- instruction regarding how it should be undertaken
- the expected change and desired outcome for the child in terms of the intervention target and goals for their development
- a set time for reviewing its impact.

4 The final stage of the cycle of involvement involves completing a **review**. This should be a dynamic, active process which looks at the activity undertaken and considers the impact made. Ideally, this process involves all those supporting the child, and if appropriate can include the child themselves. It may involve modifying or further developing the intervention where needed. Additionally, it could result in the intervention changing to a monitoring stage or inactive stage, or even a referral to another service for additional specialist support.

Monitoring stage

Often indirect practitioner involvement through periodic observation and review of the impact of an intervention over a specified timeframe

Inactive stage

No active involvement or monitoring by the practitioner occurs within an agreed timeframe

The reflective-scientist practitioner model is a cyclic process. Following a review meeting, it may be desirable to continue with the intervention for another agreed period of time before completing another review of progress made. Alternatively, a review may highlight additional difficulties which require a new assessment of concerns to be completed. The process of involvement continues in this way, with a practitioner working through the different stages of the cycle as appropriate for the child and their level of need.

Assess, Plan, Do, Review

The SEND Code of Practice (2015) proposes a similar cycle of involvement by advising that practitioners follow a systematic approach of *Assess, Plan, Do, Review* when supporting children with SEN. The document emphasises that working in this way will maximise the likelihood of a positive outcome and will more explicitly help practitioners to document progress and development.

ASSESS: identifying need

Being able to accurately define the level of need and consider what may be impacting upon this need is an important part of any assessment. Obtaining a baseline measure of functioning is vitally important to help clarify the severity of any problems and provide objective data to compare with post-intervention data to help monitor progress. Sometimes this may involve the child directly, but it can also include objective measures involving a teacher or parent and, where appropriate, the context or environment. Of equal importance is an understanding of the child in terms of any protective factors that help boost their emotional resilience. This may include understanding their strengths, special areas of interest and activities they enjoy completing in order to consider how these can be built upon to help promote self-confidence and self-esteem. Additionally, this knowledge may be helpful in facilitating change in other areas of development.

There is an increasing requirement to evidence the impact of any support offered when working in public services. This can be done by using 'outcome measures' to demonstrate change and progress. Many of the standardised measures completed during an assessment can be repeated periodically over time and therefore used as outcome measures to help demonstrate the effectiveness of an intervention undertaken. A comprehensive assessment may take time, but will provide a high-quality and informative understanding of a child's needs. Usually this will include an observation of the child within key settings and detailed discussions with adults who know the child well (including key family members and professionals from other agencies). A practitioner will better understand particular challenges the child faces in terms of their development and progression from the assessment. These can be documented on the *Challenges associated with typical milestones and transitions* form (Appendix C) and shared with key adults supporting the child.

The value of formal measurement

During the assessment	Administer a formal standardised measure and/or obtain an informal measurement of presenting concerns to determine the **baseline level of need**.
During the intervention	Repeat the same formal standardised measure and/or informal measurement of presenting concerns measured during the assessment at regular points during the intervention process in order to determine if **progress is being made**.
During the review	Repeat again the same formal standardised measure and/or informal measurement of the initial presenting concerns in order to establish if **outcome goals have been reached.**

Appropriate measures of need

Youth in Mind proposed the Strengths and Difficulties Questionnaire (SDQ) (2012) as a valuable tool to help assess and understand a child's profile of strengths and difficulties. The *Mental health and behaviour in schools* (DfE, 2014a) guidance for school staff recommends that wherever possible and appropriate, schools should use this tool to gain a better understanding of a child's profile and ascertain if they may have mental health needs that require input from specialist practitioners. Whilst schools are not expected or recommended to make a mental health diagnosis themselves, it is valuable for them to assess a child's mental health presentation and any emotional needs they may have in order to establish what will be an appropriate helpful role they can undertake. If the child's needs are significant, the school assessment can help support a referral to local specialist mental health services.

Additionally, schools may wish to complete a Common Assessment Framework (CAF) (DfE, 2011) with a child to help them better understand a complex presentation. This assessment will inform the type of support that the school, as well as other professionals outside the school setting, may be able to provide in order to more effectively support the child. This may also be the most appropriate course of action to undertake when an SDQ is not the right assessment tool to complete with a child. A CAF is usually initiated when there is concern expressed about a child (such as worries over emotional wellbeing or a lack of progression) and the needs of this child are beyond the support offered by a single setting and require multi-professional collaboration and consideration. A CAF helps by ensuring that effective communication between allied local services and professionals occurs so a more integrated and seamless provision of support can be developed.

Completing a focused observation using a tool such as the Boxall Profile (Boxall & Bennathan, 2014) can provide greater information about a child's development and acquisition of skills which will help support their learning. In this way, skills and strengths seen in and commonly used by the child can be enhanced whilst those needed to facilitate learning yet identified as absent can be targeted within a focused intervention. The Boxall Profile checklist has two main sections with related descriptors: the first looks at different strands of development, and the second explores in more depth any difficulties the child experiences that impact negatively upon their involvement in school.

Additionally, there are other standardised measures which look more closely at particular aspects of emotional health and wellbeing (such as self-esteem, social competence and emotional expression) and these can also be utilised to better explore a child's level of need and help document progression and skills acquisition. Useful examples of other standardised measures can be found in the *Measures of children's mental health and psychological wellbeing* portfolio (GL Assessment, 2015).

PLAN: building a formulation

During an initial assessment, a practitioner may often feel under pressure to advise a school on ways they can begin to better support a child with SEN who is demonstrating emotional distress. Ideally though, a practitioner should spend some time completing a detailed assessment and then have a short period of protected reflection to consider what they have learnt about the child and what might be the most appropriate steps to take next. Working through the reflective-scientist practitioner cycle helps provide practitioners with a framework to support this process of reflection, enabling them to formulate a more detailed understanding of how the child may be feeling and what may be impacting upon their behaviour, and plan an effective way forward in terms of help and support. Taking time over this ensures practitioners consider national recommendations and best-practice guidelines and therefore guarantee their practice is evidence-informed. This is more likely to increase the likelihood of the proposed intervention being successful in supporting the child.

> **Protected reflection**
>
> *Contemplative time away from the school context*

In reality, the process of building a formulation is a dynamic one that should be reflected upon regularly and modified as necessary through a cycle of involvement as a practitioner learns more about the child and what is influencing their thoughts, feelings and behaviours. This 'making sense' process often involves the practitioner looking at what they have already learnt about the child from their assessment and determining what they still need to learn through further questioning and involvement. In this way, the practitioner is able to consider what the primary needs of the child are and determine what will be the most appropriate interventions and resources to use in order to bring about positive change for them. The questions they ask may form part of a hypothesis about what is happening and why, and will help guide a practitioner's next steps.

Often the most helpful activity completed when building a formulation is diagrammatically pulling together key information known about a child, using important details obtained during the assessment. This is likely to include:

- ✿ an overview of presenting concerns, difficulties and needs of the child
- ✿ details regarding what may have triggered the difficulties observed
- ✿ important key relevant information regarding the child's school and home life
- ✿ strengths, skills and particular interests of the child, as well as evidence of protective factors
- ✿ any identified factors that could be maintaining the difficulties observed that would impact upon any intervention proposed.

See Appendix D for an example of how to complete this process.

Often, sharing a completed formulation with others supporting the child (including parents where appropriate) can help provide greater transparency in practice and clarify roles and responsibilities for each of the adults involved.

DO: delivering an intervention

Universal provision for all children aims to build emotional literacy and resilience through a comprehensive layered approach across schools and their supporting settings. But there is also a need for specific and focused targeted interventions for children with SEN identified as 'at risk' of developing a mental health difficulty. These interventions should have clear targets or goals which have been developed and agreed with the child wherever possible, and are measurable to ensure progress can be monitored and positive change more objectively quantified. Many interventions aiming to build emotional resilience will involve completing activities and building skills across key areas (Heaven, 2008). However, it is important that interventions are developed to meet the actual needs of the child, and therefore they may only concentrate upon one or two particular key areas of identified concern.

The likelihood of an intervention being successful is increased when a plan or overview of it is communicated to all those involved in supporting the child. This helps make certain that everyone is aware of the reasons why this intervention is important, the targeted behaviours to be addressed, the desired outcome goals, and the particulars of any strategies or techniques to be introduced.

Ensure all those supporting the child are aware of the important intervention information by sharing an intervention plan or overview.

An agreed intervention plan should include the following:

1 The behaviour or problem to be addressed through the intervention.
2 The function of the behaviour for the child and the current understanding of why this is happening.
3 Details of the goals or aims for the child as a result of this intervention.
4 Details of strategies and techniques that will form this intervention.

See Appendix E for a template of an intervention plan overview.

Working with the teacher

It is useful to provide a child's teacher with information and strategies that can help them better understand the child's needs and support them more effectively within their classroom. This can be documented in different ways and may include providing teachers with a visual overview of a child's particular areas of difficulty. See Appendix F for an example of how this may be communicated easily via an *Identifying Core Needs* form. Many children showing emotional distress may begin to struggle with their learning and consequently benefit from teachers modifying aspects of the curriculum for a period of time to help lessen the load for the child. An individual assessment with a child may also highlight a need for a school to enhance their universal provision for all children, and assistance may be required to further develop a positive school ethos and culture around supporting and promoting emotional wellbeing.

Working directly with a child

Sometimes a child may require a time-limited, outcome-focused, school-based intervention to be developed. This may look at exploring and expressing emotions, developing social skills, or building emotional wellbeing and resilience through increasing self-confidence and self-esteem. This kind of intervention can be offered to children individually or developed as part of a small-group intervention with peers.

When working directly with children with SEN there are some key general points which must be considered:

✿ Remember to give the child enough time to respond.

✿ Repeat information regularly and check understanding.

✿ Adopt a multi-sensory approach.

✿ Create interest and motivation to engage the child by developing tasks that build upon the child's areas of interest.

✿ Use a reward system to strengthen confidence.

General principles of creating the right environment for an intervention

Consider the following factors before beginning an intervention session with a child with SEN in order to increase its likelihood of success:

▪ **Timing**
Make sure the child isn't hungry, hot, in pain or tired, but is alert, happy, dry, seated comfortably and content.

▪ **Noise**
Ensure you will not be disturbed by the noise or presence of others during your session.

▪ **Distractions**
Clear away unnecessary toys and any items which may distract the child or reduce their focus on your session tasks.

▪ **Make session activities achievable**
Session activities should be achievable within the session length and realistic in order for the child to feel a sense of accomplishment and success.

Supporting specialist interventions

It is important that schools are aware of any support being offered to a child with complex needs and their family by specialist mental health services, and are able to help guarantee that any intervention strategies suggested are supported across both home and school settings. In these situations, it is particularly important that practitioners from across different services communicate regularly to help ensure the most appropriate support is being offered by the most appropriate practitioners.

REVIEW: monitoring progress

Whilst most practitioners will informally review the wellbeing and progress of a child throughout their involvement with them, working within a reflective-scientist practitioner cycle requires a more formal review process which occurs periodically. These formal reviews provide an opportunity to reflect upon the support being offered to a child and consider whether it should continue as it is or be adapted as the child develops and their presenting needs change. Additionally, it acts as a forum for the adults supporting a child to come together, including specialist practitioners from different services as well as parents and key family members. This gives them the chance to consider their own roles and responsibilities within the network of care.

Any formal measurements of progress, including those completed as part of the assessment to provide a baseline of current functioning (i.e. strengths and identified areas of need), should be repeated and discussed in the formal review meeting to help inform the review process. It is important to be confident in decision-making during a review as this process helps any unforeseen problems to be detected early so that necessary adjustments to an intervention can be made. Regular reviews can be held as and when desired to help support open communication and build greater accountability by ensuring interventions are being delivered as agreed in previous meetings.

The main purposes of a review meeting are:

⚙ to formally assess the progress of the child and their school against the agreed intervention targets and goals

⚙ to modify or change any intervention strategies or techniques in light of review feedback and discussion

⚙ to consider if targeted support is still needed, or if referral to specialist services is required.

Key chapter points

⚙ *The SEND Code of Practice (2015) recommends practitioners complete cycles of support or involvement with a child with SEN through a process of Assess, Plan, Do, Review.*

⚙ *This way of working supports a framework of professional practice that is informed by the reflective-scientist practitioner model. This follows a similar cyclic process of Assessment, Formulation, Intervention, Review, which helps practitioners build an evidence-informed, effective, transparent and rigorous practice.*

⚙ *The assessment process involves an attempt to objectively understand and document the needs of the child and their school. It should establish current functioning through a measurable baseline assessment which, wherever possible, should include a formal standardised measure of the child's skills and strengths as well as difficulties.*

⚙ *During the formulation or planning stage, the practitioner should reflect upon what they have learnt and still need to learn about the child in order to better understand their needs. This will help guide and inform their planning of the most appropriate support and interventions.*

⚙ *The intervention stage can be considered within a three-layered framework:*
  1 *Offering universal support to build emotional resilience in children.*
  2 *Offering targeted support for children with identified emotional needs.*
  3 *Supporting the delivery of specialist mental health interventions for children with diagnosed mental health problems.*

⚙ *The review process is an essential part of any cycle of involvement and should occur formally on a regular basis. It provides an opportunity to monitor the progress and wellbeing of the child and consider the impact a strategy or intervention is having in order to determine if the support and resources are making a positive difference and/or need amending.*

CHAPTER 6
An intervention model to promote emotional wellbeing

Key components

All comprehensive intervention programmes aimed at building emotional wellbeing should ideally include activities that focus on five broad areas, outlined below. For primary-aged children with SEN, these can be broken down into specific skills the child can develop:

1 **Promoting self-awareness**
   - Developing confidence and self-esteem
   - Becoming self-reliant and independent
   - Recognising their own boundaries, strengths and limitations

2 **Managing feelings**
   - Learning to self-regulate
   - Becoming emotionally resilient
   - Being sensitive to the feelings of others

3 **Developing a positive attitude**
   - Building an effective learning style
   - Encouraging a questioning mind
   - Overcoming disappointments and setbacks with effective problem-solving

4 **Facilitating empathy**
   - Living and learning alongside others
   - Respecting difference and diversity
   - Showing appropriate care and concern for themselves and others

5 **Building social skills**
   - Developing positive peer relationships
   - Understanding social roles and rules
   - Knowing when and how to ask for help

1 Promoting self-awareness

The process of becoming aware of our thoughts and feelings and the impact of our actions upon other people develops throughout childhood. Very young children are often quite egocentric in their thinking, impulsive in their actions and heavily influenced and driven by their own needs and desires. They become more self-aware with emotional and cognitive maturity, with their development being heavily informed by feedback they receive from other people as well as specific cultural and environmental experiences. Becoming more self-aware helps children make better sense of their world and their position within it. This helps reduce feelings of confusion and being overwhelmed. Through interactions with other people within their environment, children begin to learn more about themselves, about what they can do and what they may need help with. This self-knowledge gives them confidence and becoming more self-reliant and independent helps build their self-esteem and empowers self-belief.

Some children with SEN may struggle to develop age-appropriate self-awareness, and may function emotionally at a much younger level than their chronological age. These children may appear quite self-focused and be unable to regulate or manage strong feelings, becoming easily overwhelmed by their emotions. Children with these struggles would benefit from working in small peer groups to help build self-knowledge and a better understanding of other peoples' thoughts and feelings and how these compare with their own. It may also be valuable to work with a child individually to help identify situations that cause significant emotional challenge in order to better understand what triggers their emotional responses. This will help the child develop alternative and more appropriate behaviours as they gain more self-control and confidence in these situations. Exercises that help build the child's awareness of their skills and strengths will also help develop their self-esteem and feelings of self-worth.

2 Managing feelings

All children need to learn to understand their feelings and to self-regulate and control the expression of these emotions through appropriate language and behaviours. This developmental process typically occurs throughout childhood, beginning in a child's pre-school years and continuing through into adolescence. Becoming skilful in emotional regulation can be significantly influenced by our social and environmental experiences, with much learning occurring through observing how others manage their feelings, as well as through the feedback we receive from others regarding our direct expressions and interactions.

This is not always an intuitive stage of learning for children with SEN, and many require focused teaching and support during key stages of development, transition and change. Helping children to make links between what is happening in their life and the feelings they are experiencing will improve their emotional literacy. Some children may need support in understanding how to recognise emotions in other people, including understanding facial expressions. Other children with limited verbal language skills may need to be guided towards appropriate ways to effectively communicate their feelings using non-verbal techniques. Some children with SEN can experience strong emotions which are confusing or scary to them and leave them feeling vulnerable and out of control. Helping the child understand more effectively what they are feeling and why, as well as providing them with strategies to gain better control and expression of these feelings, can make a significant difference to a child's sense of emotional wellbeing.

3 Developing a positive attitude

The attitude a child expresses towards themselves, their learning and relationships with other people, as well as towards their life in general, is markedly influenced by their ability to self-reflect, be self-aware, and manage and understand their feelings. A child who is comfortable in their knowledge of their own strengths and limitations, who values and respects themselves, and has developed good emotional intelligence and control is likely to feel confident regarding their own abilities to try new things and eager and motivated to learn. Additionally, the actions and opinions of other people can also significantly influence a child's attitude towards life. Children who are nurtured, praised and positively directed to try new activities are more likely to become actively involved in them and feel motivated and enthusiastic about learning.

If a child with SEN is not encouraged to become self-reliant and independent, perhaps due to concerns regarding their safety or perceived ability or potential, they are less likely to have the experience of being able to make their own decisions and have control over what they do and how they do it. Being in a context where people have a low expectation of them is likely to lead a child with SEN to underachieve and consequently they may not reach their full potential. This can lead them to experience feelings of frustration and dissatisfaction, which are sometimes demonstrated through a range of challenging behaviours. For children with physical or cognitive limitations, especially those in mainstream settings, needing support to complete tasks that their non-SEN peers can complete independently can negatively impact upon their self-esteem and sense of mastery. If a child with SEN is demonstrating a negative attitude at school, practitioners need to be sensitive to the complex factors that may be influencing this attitude, and consider how the child can be supported to gain experiences of success and positive achievement which will help build their self-esteem and sense of self-worth.

4 Facilitating empathy

Developing empathy is an important aspect of building good emotional intelligence. It involves being aware of and understanding others' feelings and concerns, and knowing how to respond appropriately and sensitively to these. Like many skills, developing empathy for someone else is a quality that develops over time through early and middle childhood. Very young children are often motivated and driven by their own thoughts and feelings and their lack of theory of mind development means they may struggle to demonstrate appropriate empathy. However, through observation and imitation of positive pro-social role models, most children naturally begin to recognise that other people as well as themselves have thoughts and feelings. They learn that these should be valued and considered, and begin to show genuine concern and care for others. The child's increasing knowledge of and vocabulary regarding emotions and their impact upon how they think and behave helps them develop a deeper understanding of everyday experiences and situations.

Children with SEN may struggle to instinctively develop appropriate empathic skills and may need direct support and teaching in this area. Cognitive difficulties may result in a child demonstrating 'mind blindness' towards the feelings of other people. They may struggle to understand the complexities of some social situations and so find it difficult to know how to respond appropriately to others' responses. Targeted learning through modelling of appropriate behavioural responses to hypothetical situations involving other people can help build a child's social understanding and develop their empathy. Building opportunities for developing emotional language and communication skills in everyday activities and linking these to the actions of other people will help support a child with SEN further. Holding discussions which recognise and support the fact that different people think and feel different things in the same context will also help develop a child's emotional understanding.

5 Building social skills

Being able to form and maintain positive relationships with others is an essential aspect of developing good emotional health for the majority of people. Central to this is the acquirement of important social knowledge and understanding of social rules which help guide and inform our own behaviour and responses. These are lifelong skills which help us progress successfully through childhood and adolescence into adulthood. Through learning and play activities, children are presented with ongoing social opportunities to observe, practise and develop their social skills. They learn the rules of social etiquette, how to negotiate and problem-solve when challenges occur, and realise the impact their own behaviour and actions have upon their developing relationships.

McFall (1982) offers a useful definition of social skills, referring to them as the 'specific behaviours that enable a person to be judged as socially competent by others on a particular social task'. These behaviours can be divided into macro-level and micro-level social skills, both of which are highly important during effective social interactions.

Macro-level social skills	Micro-level social skills
<ul><li>Greeting appropriately</li><li>Asking for help</li><li>Joining in with others</li><li>Giving and receiving compliments</li><li>Competently ending and starting conversations</li><li>Dealing with disagreements</li><li>Expressing feelings</li></ul>	The appropriateness of the:<ul><li>amount spoken</li><li>tone of voice used</li><li>volume used</li><li>eye contact made</li><li>non-verbal body responses such as head movements (e.g. nodding) and gross motor movements (e.g. fidgeting).</li></ul>

Many children with SEN struggle socially and require a significant degree of facilitation and support in order to make friends and maintain positive relationships. Some struggle with simple tasks such as being able to share or take turns, whilst others need more support to help them understand social complexities such as how to know when someone is taking advantage of them. Not all children desire friendships and some children, such as those with autism disorders, may prefer their own company and find many social relationships anxiety-provoking or unimportant. Others may be desperate to make friends but find their cognitive limitations, physical or health difficulties, or problems with language and communication have a negative impact upon their social development. Small intervention groups which aim to build social skills can be successful in teaching children with SEN how to understand and develop their social abilities. Many resources are available to help meet identified social needs, although they may need to be adapted and personalised to better meet the needs of a child with SEN.

See the *Activities to promote emotional resilience* chapter for example activities that focus on each of the key skills below. The activities for each core component can be extended and developed to meet the individual needs of the child or group of children.

An emotional resilience intervention programme for primary-aged children

Core component	Key skills to develop
Promoting self-awareness	1 Be confident in recognising my strengths and acknowledging my limitations. 2 Embrace differences between people and develop tolerance in my behaviour to others.
Managing feelings	3 Learn to identify my feelings and develop ways to effectively manage them. 4 Become skilled in appropriately communicating my emotions to others.
Developing a positive attitude	5 Be motivated and open to learning. 6 Learn how to recognise my own needs and look after myself.
Facilitating empathy	7 Know how to appropriately show care and support for other people. 8 Recognise the views and thoughts of others as important.
Building social skills	9 Develop skills in sharing and turn-taking. 10 Know appropriate ways to make friends.

Pages 53–56 show examples of how a programme to build emotional resilience can be personalised and developed according to an individual child's presenting needs, using anonymised case material.

James, aged 10

Presentation of need	Possible direct interventions to build emotional resilience and wellbeing
James has a complex presentation of needs. He has moderate learning difficulties and attends a special school. *James presents with a range of concerning emotional and conduct behaviours including emotional outbursts, defiant behaviours and unpredictable mood swings.* *In the playground, James will often get into disagreements or fights and he struggles to maintain positive friendships. He is a child within the looked-after system and currently lives with long-term foster parents who also report that his behaviour at home is a challenge.* Note: *Considering James' presenting needs, it would be advisable to consider a referral to a specialist mental health practitioner (such as a CAMHS practitioner) with experience of working with children within the looked-after system as well as those with moderate learning difficulties. It is possible that James will require long-term emotional support from a specialist mental health provider in order to explore some of his emotional issues, which may relate to difficult early attachment experiences.*	**Main focus** ■ *Managing feelings* ▫ Complete targeted work looking at building James's emotional vocabulary. ▫ Help him to identify and recognise his emotional changes. ▫ Help him develop appropriate ways to communicate his feelings. ■ *Building social skills* ▫ Look at developing James' understanding of social situations. ▫ Help him build appropriate skills and strategies to facilitate peer friendships. **Additional supportive work** ■ *Facilitating empathy* ▫ Look at the impact of James' physical and verbal aggression towards others. ■ *Promoting self-awareness* ▫ Identify situational triggers that challenge James and develop strategies to strengthen his appropriate responses.

I don't like it when people laugh at me. It makes me angry.

I like to swim and go on the trampoline.

I try to ignore the other children when they wind me up.

Edward, aged 7

Presentation of need	Possible direct interventions to build emotional resilience and wellbeing

Edward attends a mainstream school and has recently been diagnosed with autism.
 	
He is reserved with his peers and is most comfortable in his own company. Edward is socially vulnerable and can be drawn into conflict with his peer group as he often misunderstands social situations.
 	
Edward shows rigid thinking and becomes easily upset and angry when he feels other people are doing the wrong thing or not listening to him.
	Main focus
	
	■ *Promoting self-awareness*
	  ▫ Consider Edward's self-identity, especially in relation to his new diagnosis and what this means to him.
	  ▫ Explore his understanding of his profile of strengths and areas of need.
	
	■ *Managing feelings*
	  ▫ Look at Edward's emotional responses in key trigger situations that are linked to particular thoughts and behaviours.
	  ▫ Look to build his strategies to help him more appropriately communicate his feelings to others.
	
	■ *Building social skills*
	  ▫ Help Edward to better understand common social situations and learn how to respond appropriately to peers in situations that confuse or challenge him.
	
	Additional supportive work
	
	■ *Facilitating empathy*
	  ▫ Help Edward to consider the impact of his behaviour upon others.
	  ▫ Build his theory of mind so he can gain a better understanding of how other people might be thinking or feeling in different situations.

April, aged 6

Presentation of need	Possible direct interventions to build emotional resilience and wellbeing

April is a popular youngster amongst her peers and has a fun-loving personality and enthusiastic zest for life. She attends a mainstream primary school and receives SEN support due to a diagnosis of dyslexia.
 	
April suffers with partial hearing loss but is reluctant to wear her hearing aids as other children have teased her about them in the past. This can lead to her struggling to complete tasks in class as she doesn't always follow instructions.
 	
April is fiercely independent and doesn't like to receive targeted individual support for her learning disability. She can become angry and frustrated by her difficulties and has regular temper outbursts.
	Main focus
	
	■ *Promoting self-awareness*
	  □ Consider with April her developing sense of self through her self-identity, particularly in relation to her areas of strengths and difficulties and how she feels these impact upon her relationships with others.
	  □ Develop strategies to help her recognise when she needs support and how to access appropriate support.
	
	■ *Managing feelings*
	  □ Explore with April her feelings about her learning needs.
	  □ Look at how she can effectively communicate and manage her frustrations in relation to her learning needs.
	
	■ *Developing a positive attitude*
	  □ Build April's self-esteem by encouraging her to recognise her strengths and positive attributes, whilst acknowledging her areas of need.
	  □ Look to build April a position of responsibility within class.
	
	Additional supportive work
	
	■ *Facilitating empathy*
	  □ Explore ways to encourage and strengthen April's caring nature towards others whilst recognising that other people care about her and want to help her when she is struggling.

I don't like it when Daddy goes away.

I like playing with my toys.

I want to look after animals when I get grown up.

Bobby, aged 4

Presentation of need	Possible direct interventions to build emotional resilience and wellbeing
Bobby has Down syndrome and attends a local primary school with enhanced provision to support students with communication and interaction difficulties. Bobby struggles to manage most aspects of his self-care without one-to-one support. He is a caring boy who desires friendships but struggles to engage with his peer group as he finds it hard to follow social rules and understand other people's viewpoints. Bobby is an only child and is very close to his mother. His father works away from home. He found it very difficult to separate from his mother when he began school and still needs a lot of emotional support and reassurance from his teacher.	**Main focus** ■ *Building social skills* □ Encourage Bobby to take part in a small social skills group within school for identified vulnerable children with SEN to help build his social language and skills and understanding of social situations. ■ *Managing feelings* □ Help Bobby to develop his emotional communication skills through exploring his thoughts and feelings in relation to common situations and trigger events. ■ *Promoting self-awareness* □ In collaboration with his mother, help Bobby to develop age-appropriate self-care skills (with agreed targets for dressing, toileting and feeding) through chaining strategies and positive behaviour management techniques. **Additional supportive work** ■ *Facilitating empathy* □ Support Bobby's developing theory of mind by introducing strategies to help him consider how other people may be feeling or thinking in different situations.

Emotional enhancement

Seligman advocated the PERMA model, which can be used to help children with SEN flourish emotionally. In this model, Seligman identifies five key elements that constitute effective emotional wellbeing. Seligman argues that a child can improve and enhance their emotional strength and resilience by developing skills in these five areas.

P	Positive emotion
E	Engagement
R	Positive relationships
M	Meaning
A	Accomplishment and achievement

(Seligman, 2011)

Positive emotion

This highlights the importance of experiencing key positive emotions such as happiness and hopefulness, and feeling connected to others and the wider world. Also important is experiencing love and nurturing care. These feelings help build our self-esteem and give us the confidence to participate in activities and try out new things. When we experience happiness and contentment our physical health is also boosted and we are more likely to experience positive social relationships. For children with SEN, it is important that everyday activities bring enjoyment and pleasure. Wherever possible, learning and activities should be fun and strengths should be celebrated and built upon.

Engagement

Like all children, those with SEN should be supported to be directly engaged with and involved in their own lives. Where possible, they should be helped to consider choices and options available to them and guided in making their own decisions. Children need to be motivated and encouraged and praised for their efforts, as well as thoughtfully challenged to continue to develop further to maximise their developmental potential. Learning is more likely to occur through direct experience, and therefore children with SEN should be involved and active participants when completing tasks rather than passive recipients.

Positive relationships

As social beings, humans rely upon relationships with others in order to feel connected to other people and actively involved in their world. Relationships meet many of our physical and emotional needs and allow us to experience important feelings associated with being nurtured and cared for. They also provide an opportunity for us to express love and support for others. Many children with SEN have difficulty in developing reciprocal positive peer relationships and need help to facilitate making friends and support in understanding important social rules.

Meaning

Seligman proposes that people feel happier and more content in life when they feel part of something and believe they are working with others towards a shared purpose or goal. Someone's emotional wellbeing can be enhanced if they feel they are undertaking something which is valued by others, and this develops their self-respect and confidence. It is important to ensure children with SEN have focus and purpose in their activities. Their emotional wellbeing will be enhanced when they successfully experience positive collaboration with another person.

Accomplishment and achievement

The experience of striving to better ourselves and achieve goals helps to build our emotional strength, and whilst it is not always possible to be successful, valuing the effort put in, time taken and progress made can be just as important. For children with SEN, it is vitally important that expectations remain high regarding what they might achieve and restrictive limits (which may negatively impact upon how they might progress) are not set. Having long-term positive goals for the future which can be worked towards in small incremental steps is a valuable way of helping a child with SEN move forward and experience a sense of pride and accomplishment in what they have achieved.

Key chapter points

⚙ *All comprehensive intervention programmes to build emotional resilience and wellbeing should include activities that look at building skills within five key areas:*

1 *promoting self-awareness*
2 *managing feelings*
3 *developing a positive attitude*
4 *facilitating empathy*
5 *building social skills.*

⚙ *Seligman developed the PERMA model to promote emotional wellbeing in children with SEN by identifying five key characteristics that underpin emotional health:*

1 *positive emotion*
2 *engagement*
3 *positive relationships*
4 *meaning*
5 *accomplishment and achievement.*

These characteristics can be strengthened and developed to build greater emotional resilience in children and help buffer against stress and known risk factors.

CHAPTER 7
Strengthening practitioners' knowledge, skills and confidence

'Good mental health is everyone's business'

In 2011, the UK government developed a directory of information to help guide commissioners in their planning and development of services promoting and supporting children's mental health and emotional wellbeing (NCSS, 2011a). An important aim of the document is to highlight how 'good mental health is everyone's business', and it explores how workforces in both universal and specialist services can be developed and supported in line with this.

Developing the workforce

This involves an evolving process of commissioning services based upon a contemporary strategic vision, which in turn helps inform the needs and capabilities of the workforce in order to deliver the required services to meet this vision. This will help ensure that mental health support and services for children are delivered by the 'right staff, with the right skills, at the right place, and at the right time' (NCSS, 2011a).

The National Workforce Programme (NWP) for Children and Adolescent Mental Health Services (CAMHS) highlights the importance of each locality developing a workforce that reflects the needs of the population it serves. It reflects upon a number of key aspects that commissioners should concentrate upon:

- Developing the mix of skills and capabilities of the workforce.
- Looking at new ways of working more effectively across professional and service boundaries.
- Creating new roles that would better meet the skills and competencies of staff.
- Ensuring training is up-to-date, responsive to need and routinely offered to all practitioners as part of a commitment to lifelong learning.

Most children with SEN and their families will have involvement from a wide range of services across different agencies. This can involve practitioners working in universal or frontline Tier 1 and 2 services, from a range of publically-funded services (such as health, social care and education) and from the charitable and voluntary sector. Therefore, universally-based practitioners need to be aware of the particular needs of these youngsters and how they can help support their mental health and emotional wellbeing as a core aspect of their role, irrespective of their professional job title. In this way, promoting the mental health and emotional wellbeing of children becomes 'everyone's business'.

Training and development across the children's workforce involves two key areas:

1 Building the knowledge and skills of staff working in **universal services** regarding children's mental health and emotional wellbeing.

2 Developing the expert knowledge and skills of staff working in **specialist mental health services**.

Supporting these developmental training aims will involve a change in cultural thinking and everyday practice for many practitioners. In general, there is a move away from rigid professional roles, dictated by job title and professional training pathways, towards building a cohesive workforce that is characterised by the skills, competencies and capabilities of its members. There is more emphasis on professionals working across service boundaries, with the needs of the child concerned determining the skill mix of practitioners involved. Professionals with specialist mental health knowledge and experience, such as those working in CAMHS, are encouraged to offer more consultation, supervision and training to those working in more universal or generic children's services. In this way, the sharing of skills and knowledge regarding enhancing mental health and emotional wellbeing in children is strengthened across all provision. There is still a vital role for specialist mental health training, and specialist mental health service providers should play the key role in supporting the most vulnerable children with SEN who have significant mental health difficulties. However, a more integrated, supportive and collaborative working model across all agencies and tiers of service delivery will help ensure that a more robust framework of emotional support and intervention is available to meet the mental health needs of all children with SEN, including those who present with less serious mental health difficulties but still require targeted mental health support.

Three influential resources

No health without mental health (HM Government UK, 2011) identifies three essential resources which will help services develop and deliver their mental health support for children, including those with SEN, more effectively:

1 The Common Core of Skills and Knowledge (Children's Workforce Development Council, 2010)

2 The Essential Capabilities (Brabban et al., 2006)

3 The Core Functions for Specialist and Targeted CAMHS (Skills for Health, 2015)

The Common Core of Skills and Knowledge

This document defines the universal qualities that should be evident in all who work with children and young people, including volunteers. In essence, these qualities provide a universal framework that can help define the core group of professional qualities found within multi-agency services.

This set of essential skills and knowledge, initially developed in 2005 and re-evaluated in 2010, was informed by earlier consultation processes which identified an ideal whereby everyone working with children and their families should have appropriate core skills in six key areas, known as the Common Core of Skills and Knowledge:

1 Demonstrate effective communication and engagement with children.

2 Have appropriate levels of child development knowledge.

3 Understand safeguarding issues and how to promote the welfare of the child.

4 Have knowledge regarding how to support effective transitions for the child.

5 Be competent and committed to multi-agency working.

6 Be skilled in sharing information and aware of the policies and procedures linked to this process.

A number of services across the UK have made these qualities key to their induction and recruitment process, and have looked to develop specific training to ensure all their frontline practitioners are competent across the skill set. However, there remains a need for all professional groups and services to adopt this core framework in order to develop a shared language and a minimum standard of expected capabilities for the whole of the workforce that supports children.

The Essential Capabilities

In 2006, children and young people were asked to consider what the most important attributes they wished to see in practitioners working in services that support children's mental health and emotional wellbeing were. This led to the development of a list of ten essential qualities as an 'ideal standard'. The list enables individual practitioners to review how well they meet these standards, and consider how they could better improve the service they offer the children they support.

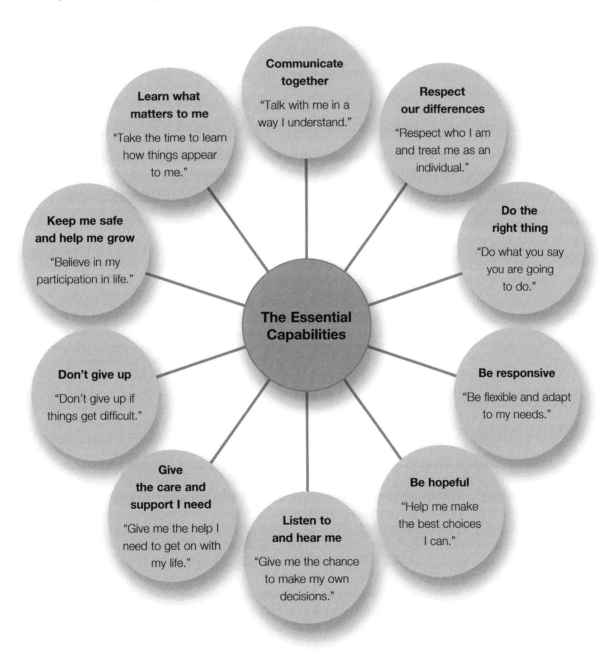

The Core Functions for Specialist and Targeted CAMHS

In 2015, Skills for Health considered national occupational standards to develop an over-arching list of nine key behaviours and competencies expected of each CAMHS worker employed within Tier 3 or 4 services. As a result, there can be greater clarity regarding local service delivery through a better understanding of roles and responsibilities, with the nine core functions helping to inform local protocols and signposting procedures. Additional role- and profession-specific proficiencies, often determined individually and by locality, will also be evident for the majority of practitioners. These will highlight any specialist or expert knowledge, skills and competencies in particular areas.

The nine core functions of a Tier 3 or 4 CAMHS practitioner are:

1 Demonstrate effective communication and engagement

- Develop supportive relationships with children and their families
- Empower children (and their families) in their own care

2 Complete specialist assessments

- Assess and advise upon the neurodevelopmental progress of a child
- Assess and advise upon the mental health and emotional needs of a child

3 Effectively safeguard and promote the welfare of children

- Understand key legislation and policies relating to child protection and safeguarding
- Assess risk of harm to children and promote their safety

4 Co-ordinate the care of a child

- Develop and co-ordinate an individual's care plan to help promote their health and wellbeing
- Implement and evaluate interventions and prepare planned discharges

5 Promote good health and wellbeing

- Provide children with information and strategies to help support their emotional wellbeing
- Support allied professionals to promote the emotional wellbeing of the children they work with

6 Support key transitions

- Consider the impact of key transitions and help prepare children to successfully manage these
- Support families and allied professionals with resources to help them prepare for upcoming key transitions

7 Manage effective multi-agency working

- Establish and maintain positive joint-working relationships with local services
- Provide clarity over own role and responsibilities and establish procedures for supporting joint working

8 Share information appropriately

- Establish confidentiality and consent procedures for the sharing of information within and across services
- Work with families to ensure information provided is appropriate and clear

9 Demonstrate commitment to professional development and learning

- Ensure own practice is informed by current legislation and best-practice recommendations and guidelines

- Support other professionals in their knowledge and skills in supporting children and young people's mental health

In addition, the Skills for Health document further highlights other important resources, including free e-learning packages that can help practitioners and services develop their knowledge and skills when supporting vulnerable children.

Developing practitioners' everyday skills and knowledge for effective working

There are many qualities that practitioners develop through their formal professional training, as well as through additional continuing professional development (CPD) and everyday experience, that help develop their working practice when supporting primary children with SEN and their families. Key to developing and maintaining effective relationships with parents is the presence of **adept communication skills**. These include the need for practitioners to be unambiguous and clear in their language, to be able to modify what and how they are communicating depending upon their audience, and to know how to remain calm and non-defensive in difficult or challenging situations. Effective listening skills and being empathic and non-judgemental are also essential components of respectful and meaningful communication.

It is also of vital importance for all practitioners that they develop a **strong and appropriate professional identity**. This involves being aware of what their role and responsibilities are and where their boundaries lie in order to maintain a supportive but professional relationship with children and their families, and also work colleagues. This is something that can be particularly difficult to balance when working with children with SEN, as many practitioners will be involved with families for a number of years, often in intensive ways and through challenging times. However, it is prudent for practitioners to remain clear about their focus and involvement with any particular family they are supporting, and they should remain aware of what is professional, appropriate and effective input for them to offer.

It is likely that when working with children with SEN, a practitioner will increasingly be involved in **multi-agency liaison and consultation**. Many children and their families have a number of professionals involved in offering them a range of supportive services, and it is essential that a practitioner is aware of who is involved and for what purpose, not least to help clarify and determine their own role. Liaising with allied colleagues from different services and sections of both public and private sectors can bring its challenges and often requires determination and persistence in order to maintain effective working relationships and communication. The issue of consent must be considered, and it is important that a practitioner has parental consent to speak with other professionals and is aware of their school policy on how to gain this consent.

Working with children with complex needs often involves practitioners having to **develop their professional skills and knowledge** of particular conditions, possibly through CPD activities or through more formal training. Additionally, it is necessary for all practitioners to be fully conversant with any relevant current legislation and national policy, as well as any local authority (LA), service or school requirements that must be adhered to. This will ensure that a practitioner is committed to professional lifelong learning and that their work is informed by contemporary best-practice guidelines and recommendations.

Key chapter points

⚙ Better mental health outcomes for children and young people: a resource directory for commissioners *(NCSS, 2011a) looks at the impact of developing a skilled workforce across both universal and specialist services on meeting the mental and emotional health needs of children.*

⚙ *The directory contains information on a range of valuable resources which will help develop emotional and mental health expertise in practitioners supporting vulnerable youngsters. It highlights three key resources that all practitioners (from any service or setting) should be familiar with:*

1 *The Common Core of Skills and Knowledge*
2 *The Essential Capabilities*
3 *The Core Functions for Specialist and Targeted CAMHS*

⚙ *In order for practitioners to work effectively, it is vital that they regularly consider how their everyday skills and knowledge can be enhanced to better support children with SEN and their families. A range of core and specialist skills can be targeted through a process of CPD. This process of lifelong learning helps ensure that practice is dynamic, responsive and contemporary, and as such is better able to meet the needs of vulnerable children.*

CHAPTER 8
Partnership working with parents and vulnerable families

There is a wealth of evidence highlighting the crucial role a child's early home life experiences play in laying down the foundations for positive emotional development and future life successes. There is much research, such as that of Howe et al. (1999), to suggest that an infant is more likely to develop healthily, show appropriate emotional regulation and become skilled in social communication if they are cared for in a safe, warm and responsive manner. School-aged children are more likely to be ready to learn, achieve, attain their developmental targets and develop positive peer relationships when they have a home life which is secure, nurturing and stimulating. More specifically, there is a strong body of evidence, including research by Goldberg (2000), that suggests that the level of care that an infant or young child receives is highly influenced by their key carer's own level of sensitivity, insight, attitude and emotional resilience. Children who experience negative parenting and have significant early life adversities are at an increased risk of developing mental health problems in later life, and have poorer outcomes across all key measures of development and achievement (HM Government UK, 2011).

Parental stresses and strains

Many families of children with SEN go through a daily struggle to care for their child and help them learn new skills. A number of studies suggest that parents of children with SEN are at a high risk of feeling isolated, distressed and depressed. There are many factors that impact upon these feelings. For example, children with SEN often have a complex developmental and medical history and can struggle to achieve age-appropriate milestones. This may mean that they are more challenging to support and care for than a child without SEN, and parents and families of these children may require additional assistance and specialist input to help support their child's development, strengthen relationships and maintain general family functioning. The complexity of caring for their child can leave many parents exhausted, with their capacity to parent effectively significantly compromised by the impact of their child's challenging demands. Furthermore, families of children with complex learning and developmental needs may also have to modify their expectations regarding what their child may achieve and how they may develop, and any long-term future plans for the family can often appear uncertain and/or may need adjusting (Drabble, 2013).

Developing a positive working relationship with a family

It is valuable to consider how a school engages with parents of children with SEN and aims to build positive collaborative relationships centred around the achievements and wellbeing of the child. For some, this relationship is fairly easy to achieve as many parents of children with SEN are proactive and enthusiastic in their input into their child's learning and supportive of the input received from school. However, this relationship can be harder to establish with other families. National policies and best-practice recommendations, as highlighted in the *Mental health and behaviour in schools* report (DfE, 2014a), indicate that children with SEN are more likely to achieve and develop robust emotional wellbeing when their school works positively alongside their parents and families.

There are a number of factors influencing the level of engagement a parent experiences with their child's school and a number of ways in which this engagement can be facilitated and strengthened.

Barriers to engagement

Many factors influence how involved a parent becomes with a school. Some key influential factors that may reduce their involvement include:

- a parent's own experience of schooling being negative
- low self-esteem and uncertainty about how they can help
- competing demands and time pressures
- being unclear about what role they can play in school
- limited parenting capabilities and skills.

At the same time, a number of factors will exist within the school that will influence how engaged a family becomes with them. Some of these are linked to the wider context and culture whilst others are influenced by individual practitioner qualities. Some key factors that may reduce family involvement include:

- few precedents or existing opportunities to facilitate engagement
- policies that are unclear about the boundaries and expectations of working with families
- competing demands and time pressures for practitioners
- uncertainty regarding what role a family could play
- if previous involvement with the family has been difficult.

Strategies to enhance engagement

If a particular family is not engaging with a school, an individual appraisal is needed to fully understand why. However, there are a number of universal strategies that could be employed that would help improve the likelihood of parents of children with SEN feeling that they could become more involved in their child's education and development. For example:

- Consider offering some drop-in coffee and consultation sessions.
- Develop some practical hands-on workshops around commonly-faced difficulties.
- Invite other practitioners who support parents into school to help bridge the gap between home and school life.
- Have regular 'stay and play' sessions, or develop similar activities that invite parents into school.

☼ Develop volunteer opportunities for parents within the school with clearly defined projects or targets.

☼ Enhance regular verbal and written home–school communication (e.g. periodic phone calls, drop-in feedback and support meetings, notice boards, emails, newsletters).

Some settings have found that developing opportunities for children and parents (or members of the wider family group) to learn a new skill together has helped bring parents into school and provide time for them to chat and introduce themselves to each other. Sometimes targeting particular groups (such as grandparents or fathers) through themed activities can also help improve engagement.

Developing targeted parent support

There are many different examples of good practice for practitioners to consider that will enhance and strengthen a supportive working relationship. Many of these emphasise the vital importance of getting communication between schools and parents right as a key building block to developing positive reciprocal relationships. In 2010, the DfE funded a five-year independent research project carried out by the National Academy of Parenting Research (NAPR). This research assembled a list of successful parenting programmes that were rated against established standards for best practice as well as for their level of effectiveness.

Families and Schools Together (FAST) is one of these programmes. This eight-week programme for parents of primary-aged children looks to build parents' skills and competence in supporting their children's social behaviour and emotional wellbeing, as well as help strengthen their own self-esteem and confidence. Each session is split into two parts. The session begins with the parents and children working together to complete a series of tasks. This is then followed by the parents and children working separately from each other, allowing the parents some reflective discussion time alone without their children being present. Follow-up monthly parents' sessions ensure further consolidation of skills developed as well as an increasing likelihood of parents feeling supported and involved in their child's schooling.

The main principles that guide the initiation, delivery and successful outcomes of FAST are:

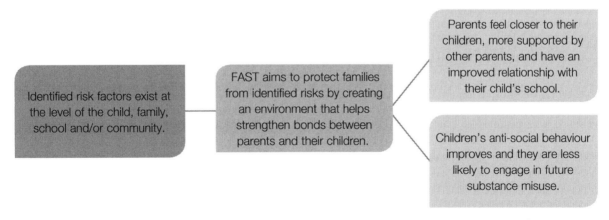

Informed by *Overview: National Academy for Parenting Research (NAPR)* (DfE, 2010)

Other models of family support that exist outside of education can also help inform how a school can support its parents of children with SEN. Much can be learnt from these models regarding how agencies can work more effectively together, and how practitioners can work more effectively with families.

One of these models of support is the Troubled Families Programme. In 2012, the Department for Communities and Local Government set out a guide for good practice when working with 'troubled families', defined in the report as experiencing at least three out of these four key criteria:

1 The family has children who are involved in youth crime or anti-social behaviour.

2 The family has children who are regularly truanting or absent from school.

3 The family has an adult on out-of-work benefits.

4 The family receives high levels of financial support from the taxpayer.

Families who fulfilled these criteria were then offered a programme of co-ordinated support. Over a three-year period, nearly 120,000 families were supported through this programme.

The guide for good practice identified five key features of supportive interventions which were the most effective in helping these 'troubled families':

1 Having a named dedicated worker for each family.

2 Offering practical 'hands-on' support when needed.

3 Having practitioners who were persistent, assertive and appropriately challenging to the family when needed.

4 Taking a whole-family approach to consider the needs of all family members.

5 Practitioners and families working together towards an agreed common purpose.

These supportive interventions found that focusing upon the whole family led to a greater understanding of the depth of need and origins of many of the dysfunctional behaviours observable in the child and the family. This led to a more targeted intervention which often involved looking at family relationships, ways of developing positive communication styles, and working with parents to set boundaries and develop warm and nurturing relationships with their children. The positive long-term impacts of the intervention helped not only the family in terms of their wellbeing and functioning, but also reduced the cost to local public services over time due to the family's reduced need for ongoing interventions and involvement with a range of service providers.

Key elements of parents' support groups

Vulnerable and fragile families more effectively support their children if their parenting skills, confidence and capabilities are developed through focused training and support. Successful parents' programmes appear to build parents' knowledge and skills by helping them to:

✿ enhance their own self-awareness and self-esteem

✿ develop appropriate expectations for their child

✿ build a greater understanding and empathy for family members

✿ instil positive disciplinary techniques in the home.

Many parenting groups spend considerable time reviewing feelings, including the process of communicating emotions (such as the release and control of difficult feelings) and the impact of praise and criticism. The groups also introduce parents to a vast array of strategies and techniques that parents can use within the family home to effectively bring about positive changes.

Many of the most successful programmes share similar aims and outcomes through building and strengthening parents' knowledge and skills.

Parent group aims and outcomes

Become more self-aware as parents through understanding the impact of our own childhood upon how we parent our children and considering how this influences our relationships. By being sensitive to our own needs and feelings, we can nurture ourselves and so be more likely to be able to care for and support others.

Recognise that children are individuals and will grow and develop in their own way at their own pace. Learn to match our parental desires and expectations for our children with what they have the potential to develop and can actually do, and value each small step of achievement.

Building positive and nurturing relationships with children as confident and caring parents

Be sensitive to and accepting of the thoughts and feelings of our children in order to better understand their experiences of the world. Children who are shown care, empathy and respect are much more likely to give it back to others.

Provide appropriate and clear boundaries for children to help them feel safe and respected. By giving greater attention and focus to positive behaviours in our children through praise and reward, and offering choices and responsibilities, the occurrence of negative challenging behaviours will lessen.

Informed by *The Nurturing Programme* (Bavolek, 2003)

Working directly with parents

When speaking with and developing a positive working relationship with a family, there are some key areas that a practitioner may benefit from considering to help better understand how the family functions. This will help them more effectively identify the family's strengths and needs, and inform their role in supporting and advising the family regarding their child with SEN. A practitioner should try to determine the answers to these questions:

- ✿ What is the impact of the child's difficulties upon the family?
- ✿ Which protective factors can be identified within the family system?
- ✿ Who else is involved in supporting the family?
- ✿ What does this family want and what do they need?
- ✿ Which risk factors can be identified within the family system?

Informed by *Report of the children and young people's health outcomes forum – mental health sub-group* (DH, 2012)

Best-practice checklist for practitioners working with parents of children with SEN

1 Be sensitive to the parents' understanding and expectations of their child. They may have a different understanding of their child's levels of ability and difficulty than you do.

2 Reflect upon the parents' experience of their child's school to date and whether this may impact upon their relationship with the school or you as a practitioner. Challenging or difficult past experiences could lead parents to initially feel untrusting, intimidated, uncertain, angry, unresponsive and/or rejecting. These feelings may need to be acknowledged and worked through if the parents are going to develop a positive and collaborative relationship with you.

3 Try to always value the child as an individual and holistically by considering all aspects of their development and functioning, not just those linked to academic or statutory curriculum attainment and progress.

4 Talk regularly with the parents about their child's emotional wellbeing and give examples of how the school is looking to build their emotional resilience. Be sensitive to the likelihood that this may include unfamiliar language or concepts for some families.

5 Wherever possible and appropriate, encourage the parents to consider how they can further build upon strategies you are employing within the school in their family home to strengthen interventions and goals and increase the transferability of their child's skills.

6 Establish with the parents what information they need to share with their child's school on a regular basis, as well as what information the parents would like the school to share with them.

7 Consider whether weekly or fortnightly drop-in times can be offered to parents of children with SEN, at least when relationships are newly developing, to help encourage regular two-way effective communication. This also ensures parents have a timely forum for sharing concerns, and provides a supportive opportunity for groups of parents to get to know each other in an informal but helpful way.

8 Consider how you communicate with the parents about their child, both in writing and verbally. Ensure that you highlight strengths and progress achieved as well as areas of need to target for possible intervention.

9 Establish with the parent what style of communication they would prefer and how often (e.g. weekly email, fortnightly phone call, daily comments in journal or diary). Make sure this is realistic to achieve when bearing in mind time restraints and the busy demands many practitioners face.

10 Ensure that communication is reviewed and its impact assessed periodically to establish that there are no misunderstandings about what has been written or spoken about.

Engaging with external agencies

It is vitally important that schools are aware of the wide range of services available within their locality that can help support families with children who have SEN, including those that deliver specialist mental health support. The local authority (LA) should be able to provide detailed information about these services through their local offer (LO). These services, from a number of different agencies across health and social care and within the wider education system, can offer specialist expertise to support a family as well as consolidate and compliment the work undertaken in the child's school. They should include voluntary and charitable services as well as those offered within public services. Key material made available for families should include information about Child and Adolescent Mental Health Services (CAMHS), social care, and children's centres.

CAMHS

Community-based generic CAMHS teams work predominantly across Tier 3 and offer a range of assessment and therapeutic intervention services within geographical localities. Additionally, these multi-disciplinary teams offer support into Tiers 1 and 2 through consultation, advice and support and training events. The criteria for acceptance into the services, size of teams and type of work undertaken by them vary enormously from locality to locality. However, most CAMHS teams will offer some support to school staff through consultation on a case-by-case basis and/or through regular professional training events. Additionally, CAMHS offer support to the parents and families of children, and many teams run therapeutic groups (for children and/or their families), often delivered jointly alongside colleagues from other services.

For children with SEN and mental health issues, the role of generic CAMHS in supporting their care is, unfortunately, often uncertain. Some parts of the UK have CAMHS teams which specialise in supporting children who have significant learning needs and mental health concerns, and these teams often play a vital and pivotal role in shaping the support network around the child. In other parts of the UK however, the specialist mental health services for children with SEN are under-resourced, and many families and schools report that they often struggle to get the expert mental health input they require for a child.

Social care

Social services look to offer a comprehensive range of support and care packages for families and children with SEN. Social workers often play a leading role in safeguarding and therefore support and work with the most vulnerable and needy members of society. They work collaboratively with other professionals to help support and empower families to achieve the best possible outcomes whilst considering individual needs and aspirations. Within a context of legal frameworks and governmental policies, social care teams also look to enhance the lives and wellbeing of individuals whose age, mental capacity or ill health limits their ability to care independently for themselves.

Social services offer a range of valuable services that families with a child with SEN may be able to access, including:

- short breaks and respite
- holiday play schemes
- adaptations for within the home
- financial advice and support for specialist resources
- early support programmes
- hands-on practical care and emotional support within the home.

Additionally, social care staff have an important role in helping support children's education. They work closely with families to help their child maximise their chances of achieving the best they can by ensuring their attendance at school is as good as possible. For families who are working with and being supported by social care, it is important that multi-agency communication between school and social care staff is effective and ongoing. This will help avoid duplication of services, ensure an accurate picture of need is understood by all professionals with a role in supporting the family, and provide a supportive and cohesive scaffolding of care for the family to build on.

Children's centres (formerly Sure Start Family Centres)

Of particular importance in the early years of a child's life are local children's centres, which can offer families a range of services to help support their functioning and wellbeing, as well as directly impact upon the development and health of a child with SEN. The core purpose of these centres is to improve outcomes for all young children and their families, particularly those with the greatest identified need. This is to be achieved through improving child development and readiness for school, developing parental skills and aspirations, and enhancing child and family health and life chances.

Since their initiation over ten years ago, children's centres now have a greater focus upon early intervention and building parenting capacity. They are ideally placed to help support general child development as well as help identify young children with SEN who may benefit from early support and interventions. Recommendations from the All Party Parliamentary Sure Start Group (2013) suggest that children's centres could become an outstanding model of partnership working where all perinatal and early years services could be focused together to help reduce replication of services and provide a tighter co-ordination of targeted care for vulnerable families.

Key chapter points

⚙ *There is a large evidence base highlighting the crucial role and impact of a child's home environment in shaping and influencing their development and future life achievements. This is especially true for a child with SEN.*

⚙ *However, caring for a child with SEN can often be challenging and demanding of a family's time, energy and emotional capacity. This leads many families to experience a high level of distress and strain which can negatively impact upon their ability to manage their child's needs and cope effectively with daily life.*

⚙ *It is crucial that schools work with parents to consider how best to support a child with SEN.*

⚙ *Many parents of children with SEN who are struggling can be supported to flourish and strengthen their skills through attending parent groups with others who face similar challenges.*

⚙ *When working closely with a child with SEN and their family, it is valuable to gain a clearer picture of their strengths and needs by reviewing:*

- *the impact of the child's difficulties upon the family*
- *the protective factors within the family system that can be enhanced and built upon*
- *who else is (or could be) involved in supporting the family from other services*
- *what help the family is asking for and what help they actually need*
- *the presence of risk factors in the family.*

Sad

✿ *Practitioners need to be aware of any local or national services outside of their own setting that could offer further support to families of children with SEN. This may include those within social care, education or health, as well as private or charitable foundations.*

CHAPTER 9
Final reflections and considerations

Supporting a model of early intervention

The report *Early intervention: the next steps* (Allen, 2011) highlights a number of key recommendations for practitioners to ensure that early intervention services which support the emotional wellbeing of children and young people of all ages and abilities are fully commissioned and developed throughout the UK. At its heart is a preventative primary emphasis, which aims to change the culture of responding 'with a late reaction to social and emotional problems' and ensure that early intervention is at the centre of all developmental government policies.

The report recognises the difficulties of establishing a culture of service delivery that embraces preventative activity at the heart of its provision rather than being led by reactionary responses to presenting need. In these challenging financial times, it is also difficult to develop a vision for an ideal service delivery which is not significantly impacted by limited resources and increasing financial restraints. The successful development of services which embrace early intervention will require creative and visionary leadership within central and local government, service providers and commissioning services. There is strong support in favour of developing a nationwide provision of early intervention core services. This must be part of the vision for the future if we are to fully support children (including the most vulnerable and those with SEN) and their families during the vital stages of their development. It is crucially important that practitioners working with children with SEN prioritise how they can more proactively look to develop high-quality, effective and timely support to enhance children's emotional health through their own routine practice and specific service, context or setting provision.

Learning from school inspection reports

In 2013, the Office for Standards in Education, Children's Services and Skills (Ofsted) reviewed the impact of PSHE teaching through evidence from their inspections in primary and secondary schools and an online survey of young people. Their report, entitled *Not Yet Good Enough*, highlighted that over a third of schools were found to require improvement in their teaching relating to personal, social and emotional health and wellbeing.

The document noted that:

> ✿ Sex and relationship teaching in primary schools was often dominated by themes

relating to friendships and relationships, with not enough emphasis on preparing pupils for the physical and emotional changes linked to puberty.

⚙ Only half of the primary schools involved in the study taught how to stay safe, especially online, and many pupils needed more opportunities to practise and apply skills they had learnt in everyday situations.

⚙ 42% of primary school teachers identified that they required additional support and direction with teaching sensitive subjects, with many subjects (such as those concerned with mental health and emotional wellbeing) not being covered because of a lack of teacher confidence.

⚙ Many primary schools had poor assessment procedures in place for learning associated with PSHE teaching, and few had a robust framework for coherent teaching that was built upon across key stages. Additionally, the management and governance of PSHE within a third of primary schools was considered inadequate.

However, notable strengths were highlighted in some schools. Those that supported pupils with SEN with bespoke lessons for particular PSHE topics and those that involved outside specialist speakers for discrete topics were noted as providing a higher-quality learning environment. The report sends a clear message to schools, including those which provide support to children with SEN, showing that making small adjustments to current PSHE provision can bring about significant beneficial changes for children.

> *Children with higher levels of emotional, behavioural, social and school wellbeing on average have higher levels of academic achievement and are more engaged in school, both concurrently and in later years.*
>
> (DfE, 2012)

What can individual practitioners do to help?

Much can be done on a day-to-day basis within a single school, classroom or lesson which can impact positively upon the mental health of a child with SEN. All individual practitioners who work with children have a responsibility to consider the emotional wellbeing of a child in their care at all times, irrespective of the main thrust or focus of their input with that child. The reflective-scientist practitioner model can be used to help structure and inform interventions and supportive practice, providing a comprehensive and robust framework from which effective emotional provision can be developed.

Ideally, best-practice universal recommendations should form the foundation of the everyday emotional support provided by a practitioner, with a further layer of additional specialist support, resources and strategies available should a child need them. Individual practitioners should consider the setting and context in which they work and look at how they can help build and modify systems and structures to strengthen the ethos and identity of their workplace. In this way, the environment or context becomes more emotionally nurturing and responsive, which will impact positively upon the experiences of the children who come into contact with it. It is also valuable to audit current provision and review whether adjustments and developments need to be made on a periodic basis in order to support children's emotional health more effectively.

What can schools do to help?

Schools play a vital role in a child's life, and therefore they also play a vital role in promoting and enhancing that child's emotional health and wellbeing. Often they hold a pivotal central position for children and the various services that exist to support them, and are well-placed to advise on local commissioning and provision. Ideally, schools should routinely consider how they can further develop the support they offer to children with SEN to help build their emotional resilience. Most importantly, they should also review the impact of this support and appropriately modify it where necessary as the demands and needs of a child change. Schools would benefit from completing *A school's guide to enhancing the emotional health and wellbeing of children with SEN* (see Appendix A) on a yearly basis (or more frequently) to help with this task.

Whilst it is recognised that schools continue to work under immense demands with a high expectation for them to provide an effective, holistic education to all of their pupils, they cannot become complacent regarding their provision of nurturing emotional support, nor lose focus on ensuring they maintain an ethos and culture that is sensitive and supportive of promoting positive emotional wellbeing. Providing effective universal provision for all pupils, as well as targeted support for the most vulnerable, under an ethos that strives to overcome stigma and prejudice against mental health problems will have a tremendous value and impact.

The Social Emotional Aspects of Learning (SEAL) resource for schools highlights that children who have developed good skills in this aspect of personal development are likely to be flourishing in an environment which is emotionally supportive (DfES, 2005a). This useful skills-building resource looks to develop the existing support schools provide in enhancing children's emotional wellbeing through a series of topics promoting positive behaviours and effective learning. Children who are supported in this way are more likely to:

- ⚙ be motivated and successful in their learning
- ⚙ be able to form positive peer friendships
- ⚙ demonstrate valuable problem-solving skills and manage their feelings (including difficult and strong emotions) effectively.

In turn, these children are more likely to grow into confident teenagers and then valued and positive adults. As this must be every school's over-arching aim for all its pupils, including those with SEN, the importance in valuing and developing emotional provision and support cannot be underestimated.

Adopting a comprehensive model of provision within schools

Provide staff with the appropriate supervision, resources and training to support children's emotional health effectively.	▪ Look at MindEd and Counselling MindEd (both free online training tools), and other similar resources to help build knowledge and skills. ▪ Take advantage of training opportunities and resources available within your local specialist mental health services.
Have structures and procedures in place within school to support identified 'at risk' children and those needing additional emotional support.	▪ Be committed to early intervention using evidence-based support, following a school-based assessment of need. ▪ Develop a comprehensive layered approach to emotional care and wellbeing that children can easily access and move between freely.
Know when and how to get support from outside agencies when a child's emotional needs are significant.	▪ Use the Strengths and Difficulties Questionnaire (SDQ) or a similar screening tool to help determine need. ▪ Agree pathways of local care for referrals for specialist mental health intervention and support.
Ensure a culture that values and enhances positive emotional wellbeing through robust universal provision for all.	▪ Look at ways children and their families can be more positively involved in school activities and developments. ▪ Encourage a culture where seeking help is seen as a strength rather than a weakness.

Informed by *Mental health and behaviour in schools* (DfE, 2014a)

What can services and commissioners do to help?

The Department of Health report *Closing the gap: priorities for essential change in mental health* (DH, 2014) recognises that funding constraints continue to shape the decision-making of many of those who commission mental health services, as well as determining issues regarding eligibility criteria and charging for specific services.

An increasing number of practitioners are becoming involved in shaping and determining their local provision, with many being invited to be part of steering or action groups looking to develop services. As such, it is valuable to be aware of the wider issues impacting upon commissioning services and how provision can be developed whilst holding these factors in mind. It is evident that the impact of working in a financially-stretched context creates a demanding and challenging environment from which to continue delivering high-quality, effective services for children with SEN and their families. Practitioners and commissioners of services have to think resourcefully and innovatively about their work, reviewing everyday practices and policies regularly in a bid to meet increasing needs with fewer resources. To help drive forward effective provision for children with SEN in this uncertain context, it is worth considering a number of recommended actions:

⚙ Central government should consider completing an independent analysis looking at the impact of the austerity measures upon children's services within both the public and voluntary/charitable service sectors, with particular reference to those supporting needy and vulnerable children (including those with SEN) and their families. This analysis would help inform future spending and recommended commissioning, and therefore ensure that obtaining the best outcomes for children with SEN is the key aim of service provision, rather than new service developments being dominated by financial restraints and limitations.

⚙ Key drivers at a local level (such as the Health and Wellbeing Boards and Local Authority (LA) commissioners) should consider how to actively engage and work alongside all service providers (including those from the charitable and the voluntary sector) in a genuine full partnership. This would help strengthen and enhance the position of all who offer support to children with SEN and their families.

The Young Minds (2011) briefing report on funding cuts to CAMHS makes a number of valuable recommendations for the government and commissioners who are concerned about meeting the emotional and mental health needs of children. These include:

⚙ A commitment to supporting a **comprehensive model of CAMHS** with funding for this way of working a priority for all localities.

⚙ Those practitioners who hold key and influential positions within public health at both national and local level must **highlight and prioritise children and young people's mental health** and emotional wellbeing at every opportunity.

⚙ All services who work with children and young people must actively work together in a more co-ordinated and integrated way, to ensure **joint commissioning, planning and delivery of mental health services** occurs.

⚙ The **input and views of children and young people** regarding the planning and delivery of mental health services should be an essential aspect of all locality services.

⚙ A **minimum standard level of service** to support children and young people's emotional wellbeing and mental health should be set for all localities to adhere to. This will minimise the 'postcode lottery' many children and their families experience with the choice of local services available to them.

⚙ The vital importance of **early intervention mental health provision** should be highlighted, and adjustments made to current provision to ensure these essential services are available to all.

Supporting a 'comprehensive model of CAMHS'

There is an increasing recognition that all services and practitioners have a part to play in supporting the emotional wellbeing and mental health of children. This ideal has helped inform a new 'comprehensive model of CAMHS', highlighted by the National CAMHS Support Service (2011b), which considers that everyone who works with children has an important role to play in supporting their mental health and emotional wellbeing, not just those working in specialist mental health services. It views mental health as a continuum, with emotional health and wellbeing at one end and chronic and enduring mental health illness at the other. Therefore, all practitioners working with children with SEN have a role to play in positively enhancing the children's emotional wellbeing, and practitioners can see themselves as part of a co-ordinated and integrated support system. The model highlights services themed across different layers of provision, which include:

⚙ **Universal**

Working with all children with an emphasis upon promoting resilience and enhancing emotional wellbeing.

⚙ **Targeted**

Working with children with identified emotional and mental health needs who can be supported primarily through time-limited interventions.

⚙ **Specialist**

Working with children with complex, severe and persistent mental health needs who may require ongoing specialist support and services.

It has been recognised that in the UK, over 50% of adults who experience mental health difficulties first experienced symptoms during childhood. This highlights the vital need for a lifespan approach to enhancing emotional wellbeing within our society and providing appropriate mental health support and care for children identified as 'at an increased risk' of developing emotional and mental health difficulties.

(HM Government UK, 2011)

The benefits of intervening

There is little doubt regarding the benefits of supporting and strengthening the emotional health and wellbeing of all children (including those with SEN) during their primary education, both in the short term and the long term. Not only is a child with good mental health more likely to achieve at school and enjoy positive friendships, but when they leave school they are also more likely to find suitable employment and live a more productive life within their community. Additionally, research suggests that adults who have positive and robust mental health are more likely to experience good physical health and wellbeing and avoid engaging in unhelpful risky behaviours such as alcohol and substance misuse.

Children with SEN are at an increased risk of developing emotional or mental health difficulties and so it is crucial that, as practitioners, we all seriously consider our role in supporting and enhancing their emotional state. We need to feel confident and competent that we know how to do this effectively and look to develop opportunities to support children's emotional health as a core part of our daily practice. Whilst there will always be a need for specialist mental health practitioners who have undergone rigorous mental health training, there is much that non-specialist practitioners can do to help support vulnerable children. Universal and targeted strategies and interventions can make a significant difference and these can be easily implemented (and their impact monitored and reviewed) in the majority of schools, settings and services without significant disruption. It is our responsibility to develop our own knowledge, skills and competencies to promote emotional wellbeing in children with SEN, and to seek appropriate support and training (if needed) to help us undertake this role.

The short-term impact of supporting and building the emotional needs of these vulnerable young children is considerable, but we must not forget that this impact potentially has a long-term consequence for the rest of their lives. We can all make a great difference: mental health really is everyone's business.

Key chapter points

⚙️ *Early intervention is a process of working which is responsive, flexible and effective in offering timely emotional support to children with SEN and their families. There is significant research indicating the value early intervention can have by allowing practitioners and services to work in a more preventative and less reactionary way to identified need.*

⚙️ *As individual practitioners, we need to ensure that we are maximising our efforts in supporting the emotional needs of children with SEN on a daily basis. This also involves looking at the wider context in which we work and helping develop better practice and systems to strengthen our school's culture in supporting emotional and mental health.*

⚙️ *It is important that we consider not just how we support the emotional needs of vulnerable children within our school, but also look at how we can champion these needs within our community through local commissioning and the process of service development. An important part of this is having a commitment to being part of a model of 'comprehensive CAMHS' and looking at ways we can better integrate and communicate with colleagues working across all services in our locality.*

⚙️ *Everyone who works with children with SEN needs to consider how they can better support the emotional and mental health needs of this group of vulnerable youngsters in the everyday work they do. We all have a responsibility to help in this way and our commitment to better support a child's emotional needs will make a big difference to their overall development, achievement and experience of life.*

ACTIVITIES TO PROMOTE EMOTIONAL RESILIENCE

This chapter offers an example of an emotional resilience intervention programme for primary-aged children with SEN. The worksheets show examples of ways you can develop specific key skills in particular areas of emotional health. They can be personalised and modified to meet a child's developmental level (e.g. built upon and developed for a more able child, or simplified and shortened for a less able child). Similarly, the level of assistance a child needs to complete the tasks may differ and consideration will need to be given to the appropriate level of adult facilitation and support required. The worksheets can be completed as part of a focused one-to-one support package or as part of a small group intervention. You can further develop the exercises through the use of appropriate toys (e.g. role-play with small animals or puppets) or crafts (such as painting) to develop themes.

These activities will be most successful if embedded within supportive discussions with the child and individualised to their abilities and interests. Use them to stimulate conversation and help facilitate your learning about a child, their needs and their strengths. Additionally, look to incorporate some of the key strategies or skills introduced through these worksheets into everyday activities. This will help provide opportunities for practice and help the child transfer skills learnt into different settings.

This book contains only some of the worksheets included in this emotional resilience intervention programme. For the complete set of activities, please see the accompanying CD-ROM.

Core component	Key skills to develop	Activity examples
Promoting self-awareness	**1** Be confident in recognising my strengths and acknowledging my limitations. **2** Embrace differences between people and develop tolerance in my behaviour to others.	All about me Finding out all about me Promoting self-awareness The same and different game
Managing feelings	**3** Learn to identify my feelings and develop ways to effectively manage them. **4** Become skilled in appropriately communicating my emotions to others.	My book of feelings How would you feel? Tricky feelings Managing difficult feelings Feeling better
Developing a positive attitude	**5** Be motivated and open to learning. **6** Learn how to recognise my own needs and look after myself.	My learning prescription My learning tree Climbing net ladder of success My helpful bottles My helping actions checklist My helping actions flag
Facilitating empathy	**7** Know how to appropriately show care and support for other people. **8** Recognise the views and thoughts of others as important.	Showing I care My 'helping others' bag My helping hands My 'working nicely with others' rules My 'working nicely with others' reminders What happens next?
Building social skills	**9** Develop skills in sharing and turn-taking. **10** Know appropriate ways to make friends.	We can share together My sharing ladder Sharing is caring I can take turns! My taking-turns hot air balloon I know what makes a good friend I can be a good friend My 'making friends' map

Promoting self-awareness

Be confident in recognising my strengths and acknowledging my limitations

General points to consider when completing these activities:

⚙ These exercises aim to build children's self-awareness and self-esteem through helping them develop a balanced picture of their profile of skills. This involves confidently highlighting skills and positive attributes that the child has as well as exploring areas of challenge and struggle.

⚙ Ideally this task will involve key adults (including family members) who know the child well and can sensitively explore the child's development and progression with them.

⚙ Talking with the child about things that they enjoy doing and participating in will often help illuminate areas where their strengths and skills may be most obvious.

⚙ Try to make emotional links for the child regarding how they feel when they identify something they are good at and how they feel when people say nice things about their skills and strengths.

⚙ Explore areas of difficulty and challenge for the child by acknowledging that everyone has things that they enjoy and can do quite well, as well as things they can't do easily and need help with.

⚙ Alternative worksheet examples are provided to suit different children, depending upon their age and interests or preferences.

⚙ As a practitioner, use the information gained from completing these exercises to help build opportunities for everyday practice to build the child's emotional resilience. For example, use the child's identified strengths and skills when completing other activities during the day and acknowledge with the child (and others) how valuable it was that the child was able to help and had good skills in this area. Additionally, consider identified areas of need and look to build the child's confidence and skills in these areas through targeted support.

Note: For children who struggle to identify their own strengths and needs, encourage key adults who know the child well to help the child complete the *Finding out all about me* worksheet.

All about me (1)

"There are many things that I am good at and can do well."

Write or draw some of your strengths that you are proud of in the stars.

Promoting self-awareness

Embrace differences between people and develop tolerance in my behaviour to others

General points to consider when completing these activities:

⚙ These activities are designed to help children become more aware of other people's thoughts and feelings, and recognise that these may differ from their own and that this is okay.

⚙ They offer an opportunity to develop theory of mind skills through completing joint activities with another child, facilitated by an adult.

⚙ These activities can be completed in small groups with children sharing their answers when complete. This provides a chance to highlight similarities between the children as well as differences. Both should be similarly celebrated.

⚙ Children should be told at the start of each activity that there are no wrong answers and that everyone is an individual with their own thoughts and feelings which should be respected and valued.

⚙ Activity content should be adapted (e.g. extended or simplified) to meet a child's needs.

⚙ Similar activities using craft materials can be completed simultaneously with a small group of children. For example, create a mural entitled *Learning about each other*. Help each child to complete individual cut-out clouds which share information about things such as their favourite foods, clothes and sport as well as dislikes and fears. The clouds can be displayed together on a wall explicitly celebrating similarities and differences. Alternatively, get a group of children to lie on sheets of paper and draw around the outline of their body. They can then colour, draw, write and stick key information about themselves in their body shape. When complete, these 'paper children' can be displayed and their contents discussed openly.

Promoting self-awareness (1)

"You might not know this about me, but..."

My favourite food to eat is...

I really like to play...

Something that scares me is...

I feel happiest when...

I get really angry when...

Managing feelings

Learn to identify my feelings and develop ways to effectively manage them

General points to consider when completing these activities:

⚙ The aim of these activities is to help a child develop a greater understanding of their own feelings and build a valuable emotional vocabulary to aid their expression and communication skills.

⚙ The content of the exercises can be adapted depending upon the needs and abilities of the child. For children with limited vocabulary and/or understanding of emotions, it may be useful to focus upon key emotions first (e.g. happiness, sadness, anger, fear), whereas other children may be better able to understand more complex feelings (e.g. guilt, embarrassment, resentment, jealousy).

⚙ Use everyday opportunities to help the child accurately name their feelings and where possible share with them how you have come to a conclusion about what they are feeling (e.g. "I can see having to wait is making you feel angry because you have a frown on your face and you are stamping your feet.") By doing so, you will also be making important links between how the child is feeling and how they are behaving.

⚙ Ideally, children need to learn the links between their feelings and the context they are in. This helps them realise how their emotions are influenced by situational factors and begins to build their self-awareness of triggers that influence changes in their own feelings. Where appropriate, practitioners can discuss the child's behaviour with them, comment on how this might be linked to how they are feeling, and then relate this to what might be happening in their environment.

⚙ Use story books and magazine pictures to help identify feelings in others, especially through changing emotional expressions. Build a mural of happy faces and activities that often make people feel happy, and repeat this exercise for other key emotions.

⚙ Discussing feelings can be difficult for some children. Initially, it may be necessary to use puppets or soft toys to depersonalise your discussions. As a child becomes more comfortable and familiar with the subject, you will find you need your props less and can talk more directly with the child about their own emotions.

⚙ Where appropriate, share and discuss the children's answers together in small peer groups to help build their awareness of how other people may feel and express their emotions across a range of contexts.

Note: Use the examples on the *How would you feel?* worksheet to explore with the child how different people can feel a range of emotions when they are in the same situation and how other people might feel another way to us. Explore how the child currently copes with their feelings and discuss with them ways in which they could manage their feelings more effectively.

My book of feelings

There are many different feelings or emotions. Can you name some of the feelings you have and write them on the book?

Put a <u>line</u> under any feeling that you don't like having.

Managing feelings

Become skilled in appropriately communicating my emotions to others

General points to consider when completing these activities:

⚙ These activities help a child explore the experience of difficult feelings. They consider how the child currently copes with these feelings and aim to determine more effective ways of managing challenging emotions.

⚙ Some children may need support in identifying difficult feelings. It is useful to help a child reflect upon recent experiences when they have become upset or angry and help them understand what was happening in the situation to make them feel that way.

⚙ As always, it is valuable to normalise the experience of challenging or difficult feelings by stressing that everyone sometimes feels angry, frustrated, frightened or anxious, and that sometimes these feelings are hard to cope with.

⚙ Where appropriate and possible in everyday situations, help a child take responsibility for their responses to their feelings by exploring the triggers which led to an outburst, what they did and how it impacted upon others with them in a moment of post-outburst calm reflection. This can also help build empathy and a greater understanding of the thoughts and feelings of other people.

⚙ Use the traffic light system to build a greater awareness of known triggers. It should flag to the child to STOP (red), take a moment to THINK (amber) about what is happening and consider their changing emotions, and choose a more helpful way to respond, or DO (green).

⚙ Most children with SEN will need ongoing support and regular prompting to successfully generalise and implement into everyday life any strategies that come about from completing these exercises. Sharing agreed strategies with key family members will help build consistency in a child's experience and increase the likelihood of the strategies becoming embedded and part of the child's developing repertoire of skills.

Tricky feelings

Sometimes we can feel difficult emotions that are hard to keep hold of.
Write in the hats any feelings that you struggle to manage.

Developing a positive attitude

Be motivated and open to learning

General points to consider when completing these activities:

- ⚙ The aim of these exercises is to help children (and those working with and supporting them) develop a greater awareness of the factors that impact upon their learning, and increase the likelihood of a child's progression and development by strengthening their motivation and enthusiasm to learn.

- ⚙ It is important that teachers and key adults who know the child well consider what they already know about them and their capacity to learn. Considering known factors that are detrimental to the child's learning and those which enhance their potential are important to share with the child themselves to help build their self-awareness.

- ⚙ Key physiological and environmental factors should be considered as these will impact upon how a child is feeling and in turn their attitude towards learning. There may be numerous factors common to many children with SEN, although some may be personal to a particular child. Completing these exercises can begin the process of identifying these factors.

- ⚙ Children with particular hypo- or hyper-sensitivities (such as to particular sounds, sights or smells) may benefit from a more specialist assessment exploring their management of sensory responses in order to identify the most effective context for learning.

- ⚙ Build upon a child's particular preference of learning style to improve their attitude towards learning. For example, observe whether learning is enhanced when information is presented visually rather than verbally, or through tactile activities that involve direct participation, or through stimulating the full range of senses.

- ⚙ Learning is enhanced and a child empowered when they feel positively about their own abilities and are interested in the topic they are learning about. Completing exercises that strengthen a child's self-esteem and highlight their strengths by building upon their existing knowledge and interests will help improve a child's motivation.

My learning prescription

Tick (✓) all the things that you think will help you learn more easily.

- ✿ feeling hungry or thirsty ☐
- ✿ someone encouraging me ☐
- ✿ feeling happy ☐
- ✿ feeling cold and wet ☐
- ✿ someone helping me when I get stuck ☐
- ✿ feeling supported and listened to ☐
- ✿ feeling warm ☐
- ✿ lights being bright ☐
- ✿ noisy people around me ☐
- ✿ having a quiet corner to work in ☐
- ✿ feeling sad ☐
- ✿ getting praise when I work well ☐
- ✿ learning about things I am interested in ☐
- ✿ learning alongside my friends ☐

What else helps you learn more easily?

_____

_____

_____

Developing a positive attitude

Learn how to recognise my own needs and look after myself

General points to consider when completing these activities:

⚙ The aim of these exercises is to help a child with SEN become more confident and competent in recognising when they are struggling to complete a task, and to develop a strategy to help them access appropriate support.

⚙ Although our emphasis is upon encouraging children with SEN to develop skills, deal with their problems independently and become less reliant upon adult support, there will be occasions when a child requires adult input. It is therefore vitally important that we equip the child with the skills and confidence needed to access appropriate help.

⚙ These activities will build upon a child's growing self-awareness, helping to highlight key areas of challenge for them and providing an opportunity to discuss the child's current behaviour and emotions when faced with these challenges.

⚙ These tasks provide an opportunity to discuss with the child their wider support and care network, and to help identify key people the child trusts and feels able to approach for help in different contexts.

⚙ It is important to normalise the act of seeking support by acknowledging that everyone needs help from other people sometimes. Where possible, try to build a list of different key strengths of a group of children and use this information in everyday tasks to help identify one particular child's skills which could be used to help another child. In this way, a child with SEN will have the experience of both giving and receiving support which will help build their confidence and self-esteem.

Note: *My helpful bottles* can cover broad areas of need (see sheet 1) or be broken down to help explore specific needs and areas for support (see sheet 2).

Note: After completing *My helping actions checklist*, you may need to identify particular setting-dependent actions that the child needs to initiate to obtain support in specific situations. In this way, individual checklists can be developed for targeted areas of focus (see *My helping actions flag*).

Climbing net ladder of success

Write some skills that you feel **confident** about towards the top of the climbing net.

Write some skills that you **need help** to develop towards the bottom of the climbing net.

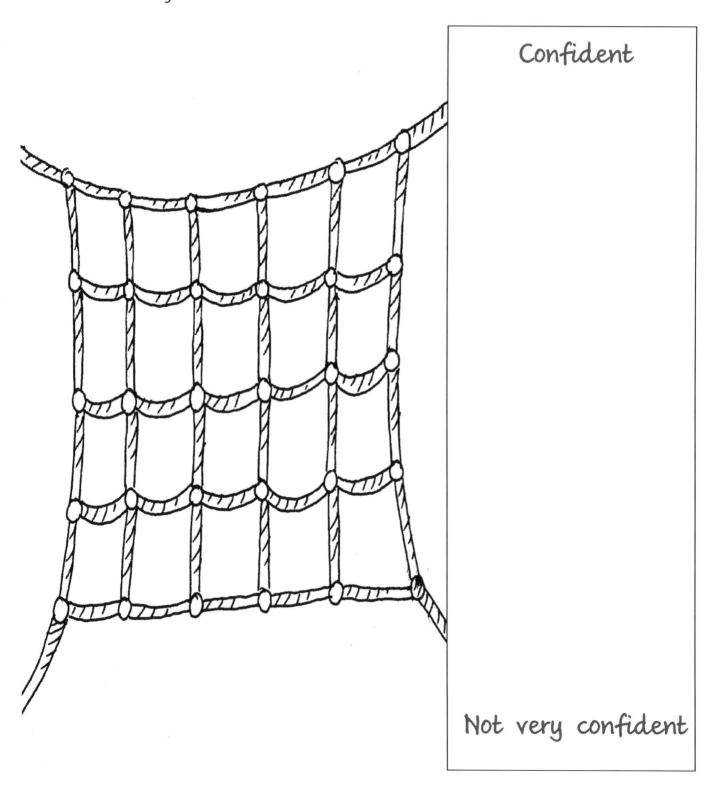

Confident

Not very confident

Facilitating empathy

Know how to appropriately show care and support for other people

General points to consider when completing these activities:

⚙ Helping a child to develop empathy involves consideration of a range of different skills. It is important to consider which particular skill(s) would benefit from targeted input and support. Stages of empathy development in children include:

■ Having *a* **greater sense of awareness** of other people by realising they have valid and important thoughts and feelings that may be different to their own.

■ Developing **good listening skills**, which lead to a child becoming less focused upon their own needs and more focused upon what someone else is saying.

■ Developing **observation skills** so a child becomes more skilled in watching other people and learning to understand what is being communicated through their non-verbal cues.

■ Developing **greater understanding of the relationship between their thoughts, feelings and behaviours** and making logical links between them (e.g. observing someone displaying angry behaviours such as stamping feet and clenching fists, and associating these behaviours with feeling angry and having angry thoughts).

■ Developing an **understanding of commonly-faced social situations** *to* reduce any confusion a child may have about what is happening and why, as well as enhancing their social knowledge and insight into how they can appropriately respond in these situations.

⚙ Developing empathic skills will help a child recognise when someone may need support. It is important that they learn what is and isn't appropriate support to give someone else to help protect their own safety, as well as develop an awareness of when the timing is right to offer assistance and how to respond if that assistance is rejected.

⚙ Differentiating between offering the right type of support for different people in different situations requires a sophisticated social understanding, which many children with SEN may struggle to acquire. Providing simple key rules which they can apply in familiar settings may be a useful compromise.

Showing I care

"Helping people shows I care about their feelings and often makes people feel better. There are lots of different ways I can show I care for others..."

When someone is crying

When someone is sad or lonely

When someone is struggling with their work

How could you help if...

Your friend fell over? _____

_____

Your mum burnt the dinner? _____

_____

Your teacher dropped their books? _____

_____

Someone you didn't know was crying on the bus? _____

_____

Someone you didn't know in the supermarket dropped their shopping? _____

_____

_____

In what ways can you help people at school?

_____

_____

Facilitating empathy

Recognise the views and thoughts of others as important

General points to consider when completing these activities:

⚙ Ideally, these exercises will be completed as part of a wider package of interventions looking at developing a child's empathy for others through building their personal and social knowledge and understanding of what might be happening in a situation.

⚙ For children who struggle with listening to other people, it can be valuable to introduce activities which can develop their listening skills through everyday learning opportunities. Linking the verbal request of listening with a physical action which is prompted and supported through visual cues in the environment can help (e.g. stating 'I need you to listen now' whilst holding your hand behind your ear and putting your finger to your lips, strengthened by pointing at a wall poster highlighting good listening skills).

⚙ Developing a child's theory of mind is an important aspect of the child developing empathy for another person. Use everyday pictures (in books, photographs or magazines) to discuss with a child what the person in the picture might be thinking or feeling and why. Where possible, encourage the child to consider how they might feel in the same situation. These discussions will help build the child's understanding and acceptance that different people might feel different things in the same situation.

⚙ Completing activities like this in small groups will help demonstrate how different children might give different answers to the same question. Encourage children to show good listening skills when others are talking, and to understand that everyone has a right to speak and provide an opinion.

My 'working nicely with others' rules (1)

Sometimes it's useful to remind ourselves of what we should do when we are working nicely with other people.

How do we show we are listening to someone when they are speaking?

_____

_____

Why is it important to listen to what other people are saying?

_____

_____

When other people are speaking to us, where should we look?

_____

_____

When we are speaking, where should we look?

_____

_____

When we are working with other people, what should we do with our hands?

_____

_____

What shouldn't we do with our hands?

_____

_____

Building social skills

Develop skills in sharing and turn-taking

General points to consider when completing these activities:

⚙ There are a number of key social skills which children may need support in developing to build their social competence and facilitate peer relationships. Two core skills involve being able to share appropriately with another person and being able to take turns without conflict during everyday tasks.

⚙ Where possible, it's valuable to help a child understand why they need to share and take turns, as well as to give them the opportunity to practise these social skills in real-life situations.

⚙ Use opportunities within everyday activities to consolidate this learning and link it to previous exercises associated with emotions and empathy. For example, if a child pushes in front of another child when queuing up, ascertain what the child who pushed in front thinks is the right behaviour to show in this situation by asking them:

- How would you feel if this happened to you?
- How do you think the child you pushed out of the way is feeling?
- What might the child you pushed out of the way be thinking?

⚙ Use visual cues in the classroom (such as posters and signs) to support sharing and turn-taking skills, as well as key verbal prompts and reminders.

⚙ Additionally, consider developing some social group rules for agreed behaviours with the children which include recognising the importance of sharing nicely and taking turns with each other.

We can share together

There are lots of different ways we can share with other people. Sharing helps us make friends and makes people feel happy.

Tick (✓) all the ways you share with others.

I share my toys. ☐

I share my sweets. ☐

I share my ideas. ☐

I share my feelings. ☐

I share people I care about. ☐

Building social skills

Know appropriate ways to make friends

General points to consider when completing these activities:

⚙ Many children with SEN need support in developing and maintaining their peer relationships. For most children, having friends is a desirable and essential part of everyday life. Friendship can bring companionship and enjoyment, help develop self-worth and identity, and provide an important opportunity for learning and skills development.

⚙ The social process of making and maintaining friendships often involves a wide range of skills, and many subtle and complex factors impact upon it. Considering this process and recognising which specific areas of difficulty a child may have will help inform the content of a focused and supportive intervention.

⚙ Making and maintaining friendships involves:

- knowing how to appropriately approach another child
- knowing how to begin and develop conversation
- being able to play and work co-operatively
- being kind (often shown through caring gestures and words)
- demonstrating effective problem-solving skills
- solving disagreements and conflict
- being able to share and take turns
- having empathy for someone else's feelings and thoughts
- being able to listen to another person
- being responsive to another person's verbal and non-verbal cues.

⚙ There is a range of social skills intervention resources available which can provide useful material to facilitate the development of some of the key skills needed when forming effective peer relationships. Whilst they may need adapting to meet the particular needs of children with SEN, they can provide a focus for individual or small-group interventions. Additional consolidation of these skills can usefully occur through everyday life, helping to generalise or embed the learning from focused and targeted sessions into the child's daily routines and activities. The key messages in the interventions should be reinforced by the child's wider setting to help develop a positive and shared inclusive culture that supports the importance of developing and maintaining friendships.

I know what makes a good friend (1)

Can you sort these descriptions into two piles?

One pile should describe someone who would make a good friend and the other pile should describe someone who might not make a good friend.

Can you think of some other ways children can be a good friend? Write or draw them in the empty boxes.

Good friend	Not-so-good friend

See I know what makes a good friend (2) for descriptions.

APPENDIX A

A school's guide to enhancing the emotional health and wellbeing of children with SEN

Consider the following questions in relation to the practice within your school, including that of particular teams and individuals. Use them to help identify areas where provision could be improved and developed to help strengthen the support available, as well as highlight areas of good practice and high-quality provision to be celebrated and shared. Think about how you can evidence your answers. Review any professional learning needs that arise from completing this checklist and identify how these can be addressed.

Rate and colour each group of questions to identify areas of need as well as areas of strength:

(GREEN) Good practice in place, no further action required

(AMBER) Some improvement and development required

(RED) Identified need, priority area for prompt action

1   Consider applying a **reflective-scientist practitioner framework** to your work. In what ways are you already working within this model of practice? What do you need to change to incorporate key aspects of this framework? How can adopting this model help improve the support your team, service or school offers to children and their families?

Rating: ( ) _____

_____

_____

_____

2 As an individual practitioner, do you need to further build your **knowledge and skills** around enhancing the emotional health and wellbeing of children with SEN? What changes can you make to your everyday practice (including the physical context in which you work) that will help strengthen children's emotional resilience? How can you champion this issue within your school? How could your school show greater commitment to supporting the emotional needs of children with SEN and their families?

Rating: ◯ _____

_____

_____

_____

3 Identify your **strengths and areas of need** as a practitioner. Are you able to meet all the demands of your role and position? What do you find challenging? What more do you need to learn about? Do you know how to maintain a professional boundary and not become over-involved in the personal dilemmas of a family you are supporting? Do you know how to be assertive but supportive in your communications? Are you able to demonstrate good listening skills and ask effective questions? How can you address any of these needs as part of your continuing professional development?

Rating: ◯ _____

_____

_____

_____

4 How does your setting support social and emotional **relationships between children with SEN and those without SEN?** What specific interventions and strategies are in place to ensure that mainstream placements for children with SEN are a positive social learning experience?

Rating: ◯ _____

_____

_____

_____

5 Consider the importance of **early intervention** and its practice within your school or setting. How can you more promptly identify children in need of emotional support and put into place effective and appropriate support within a model of Assess, Plan, Do, Review?

Rating:

_____

_____

_____

_____

6 Review the **PSHE teaching** in your school. Could children with SEN be better supported to fully access this part of the curriculum? How do you assess their learning and understanding of key PSHE teaching? Are there more effective ways to monitor their emotional and social development to help inform support and interventions offered?

Rating:

_____

_____

_____

_____

7 Consider how your school currently **recruits, inducts and trains staff** across all settings that involve children with SEN. Are the areas of expertise outlined in the Common Core of Skills and Knowledge considered in the recruitment process? How can you use the Essential Capabilities to develop and improve your practice and that of those you work with?

Rating:

_____

_____

_____

_____

8   How could you **strengthen opportunities and experiences for families of children with SEN** to help parents to:

- build their self-esteem and self-worth?
- develop more appropriate expectations regarding their children?
- become more empathic to their children's needs?
- learn more consistent and appropriate positive discipline and management techniques that they can use within the family home?

Rating: ( ) _____

_____

_____

_____

9   When working with the families of children with SEN, consider **how vulnerable families are currently supported** in your school. Do they have a named practitioner or staff member to approach and liaise with? Are they involved in making decisions regarding their child? Does your school have a policy on how to proactively communicate, support and engage with hard-to-reach or fragile families? Are there opportunities for the parents of children with SEN whom you support to come together and develop a supportive, informative group? Does your school encourage and facilitate regular parent–child joint activities?

Rating: ( ) _____

_____

_____

_____

10 Are you aware of the services that your **local CAMHS team, social care department and children's centres** offer that may be able to support the families of children with SEN you are working with? Are there opportunities for developing consultation, training or partnerships that would help your school further support the emotional needs of children with SEN?

Rating: ( ) _____

_____

_____

_____

11 Consider how you and your school work alongside colleagues within a local model of **comprehensive CAMHS support**. Are there ways you could improve communication and collaboration between services and professionals? Are you taking advantage of all available opportunities for joint training and consultation? How could you help develop a more responsive, integrated and seamless local support service for children with SEN and their families?

Rating:

12 How can you help inform **local decision-making and commissioning** regarding services to support the mental health and emotional wellbeing of children, especially those with SEN? What are the local pathways of communication that you could feed into? Are there any strategic groups that you could join or communicate with to help highlight the emotional needs of vulnerable children?

Rating:

What is working well? What are you proud of? How are you effectively supporting the emotional needs of children with SEN?

What are the practices or systems that you, your team and school feel are well-established and working well? How could you share these examples of best practice with other local schools to help develop their systems?

What needs to be developed in order to better support the emotional needs of children with SEN in your school?

Consider how you are going to develop these needs through agreed action points. Who can help you meet these needs? What resources are there available that you could draw upon? How will you monitor your progress in meeting these priority needs?

Continue on a further sheet if needed.

Completed by: _____

_____

_____

Date: _____

APPENDIX B

Checklist for practitioners and schools to enhance the emotional wellbeing of children with SEN

A reflective exercise to help audit current support and identify future actions

Name of child: _____

Completed by: _____

Date: _____

This form can be used periodically to review current provision to enhance and support the emotional needs of children with SEN and identify areas for development. Consider each of the five general factors that can all have a significant positive influence on children's emotional health and record evidence of where need is being successfully met as well as any areas needing development.

General factor	Current support and provision	Identified need and development
Promoting the child behind the disability *e.g. supporting interests; identifying strengths; developing the child's problem-solving and expressive skills; enhancing their confidence and self-esteem*		
Creating a caring community *e.g. ensuring those supporting the child are patient and sensitive to their needs and demonstrate a positive attitude; holding high aspirations for the child's progress and achievements*		
Helping the child to live a fulfilled life *e.g. building independence where appropriate; promoting inclusion; developing skills and strengths; supporting involvement in extra-curricular activities; facilitating social opportunities*		
Facilitating good physical health *e.g. considering any health needs which may impact upon a child's development and learning; helping and promoting a child's physical health and their understanding of its importance*		
Supporting development and progression *e.g. completing regular reviews of progress and development against targets set; nurturing interest for learning; building opportunities for learning and accomplishment through a child's active engagement and participation*		

Continue on a further sheet if needed.

Adapted from *Checklist of factors protective of emotional wellbeing in children and young people with SEND* (Bailey, 2012)

Proposed date for next Checklist review: _____

APPENDIX C

Challenges associated with typical milestones and transitions

Name of child: _____

	Predicted difficulties	Strategies to help
Coping with educational transitions		
Learning new skills		
Developing positive peer relationships		
Sense of self-identity and self-esteem		
Negotiating relationship changes with key adults		
Becoming independent and making choices		

Completed by: _____

Date: _____

APPENDIX D
'Making sense':
A diagrammatic formulation

Consider the below information with regards to the child you are working with. Complete the diagram opposite with key information which helps your understanding of the child.

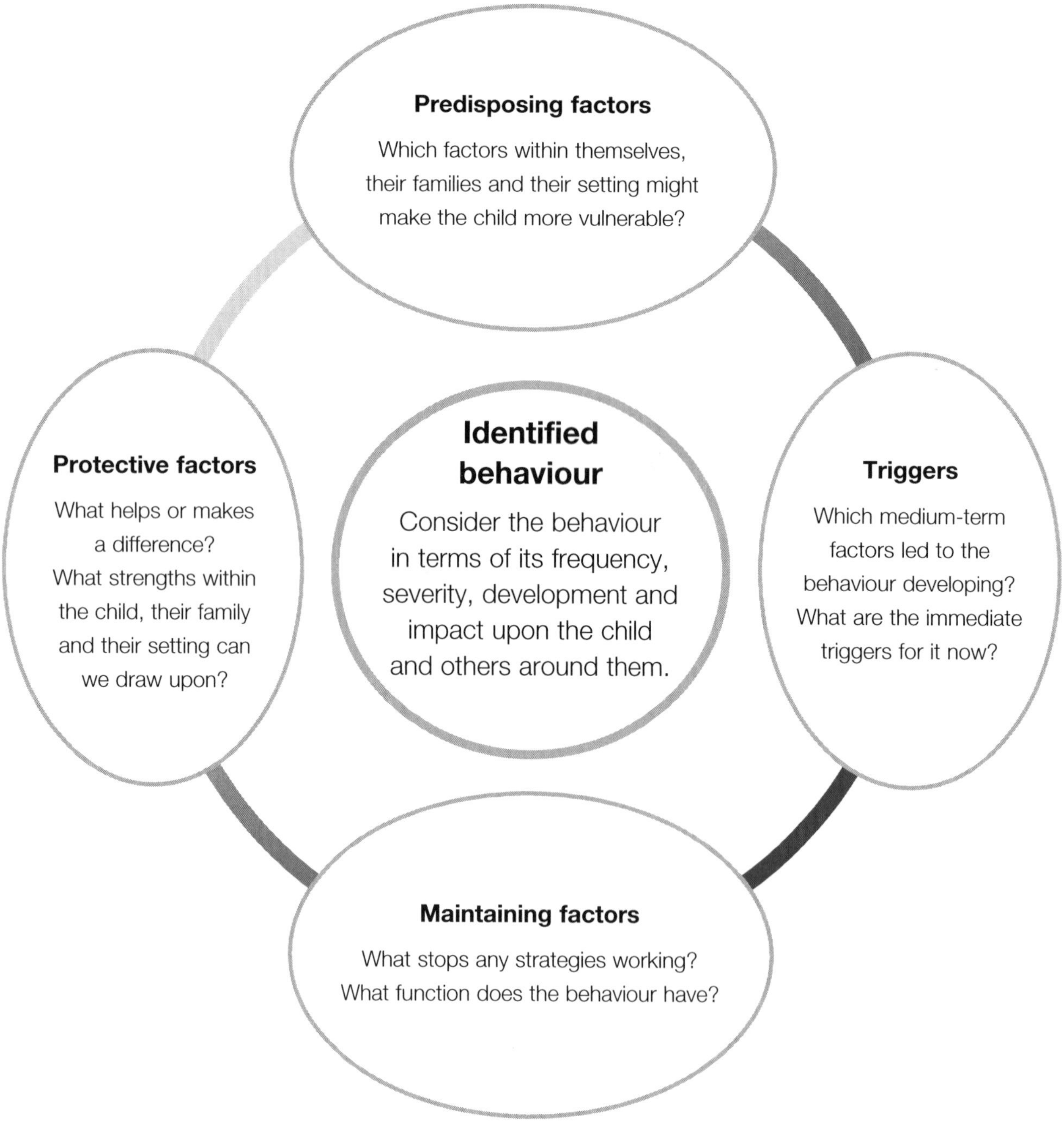

Predisposing factors

Which factors within themselves, their families and their setting might make the child more vulnerable?

Protective factors

What helps or makes a difference? What strengths within the child, their family and their setting can we draw upon?

Identified behaviour

Consider the behaviour in terms of its frequency, severity, development and impact upon the child and others around them.

Triggers

Which medium-term factors led to the behaviour developing? What are the immediate triggers for it now?

Maintaining factors

What stops any strategies working? What function does the behaviour have?

Name of child: _____

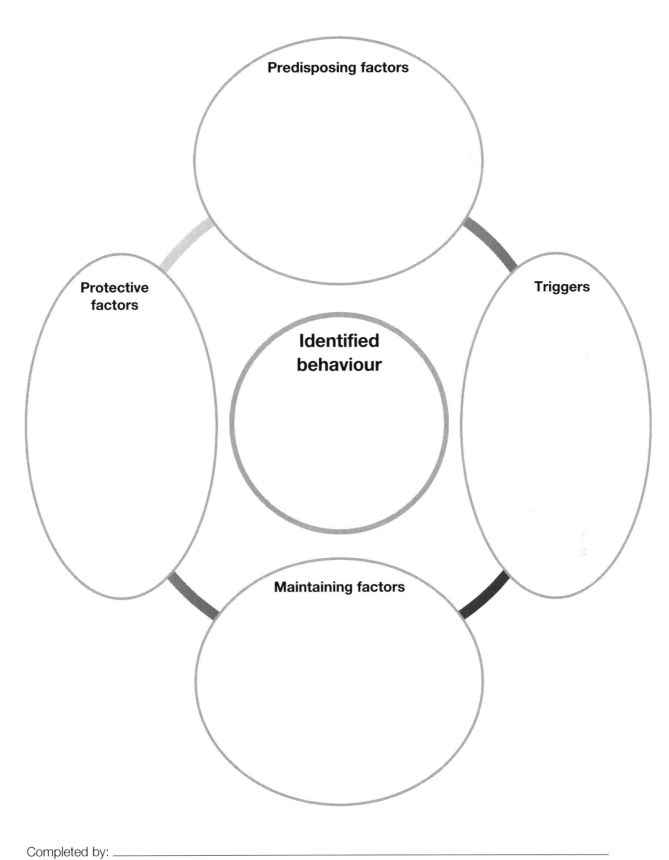

Completed by: _____

Date: _____

APPENDIX E
Agreed intervention plan overview

Name of child: _____

The behaviour or problem to be addressed through the intervention	
The function of the behaviour for the child and the current understanding of why this is happening	
Details of the goals or aims for the child as a result of this intervention	
Details of strategies and techniques that will form this intervention	

Completed by: _____

Date: _____

APPENDIX F
Identifying core needs

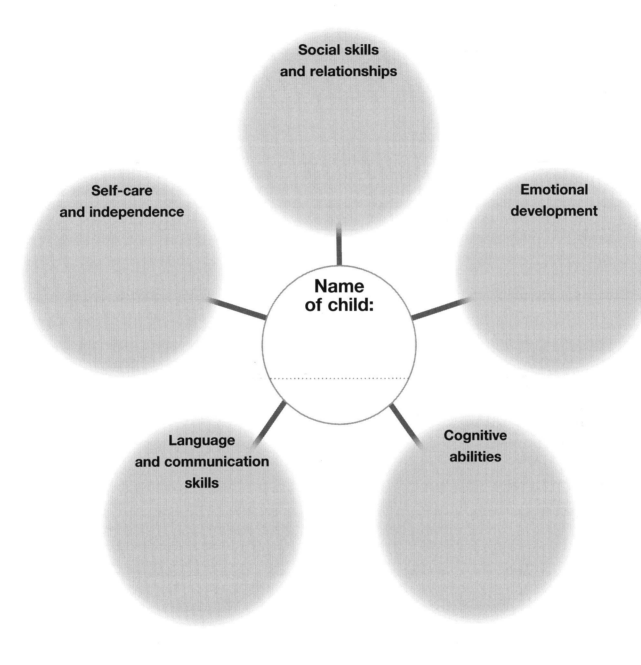

REFERENCES

Achenbach T (1991). Integrative guide for the 1991 child behaviour check list/4–18 YSR, and TRF profiles. Vermont. University of Vermont Department for Psychiatry.

Allen G (2011). Early intervention: the next steps. London. Department for Work and Pensions.

All Party Parliamentary Sure Start Group (2013). Best practice for a sure start: the way forward for children's centres. www.4children.org.uk/Files/cffc42fe-49eb-43e2-b330-a1fd00b8077b/Best-Practice-for-a-Sure-Start.pdf

Anders Y, Sammons P, Taggart B, Sylva K, Melhuish E & Siraj-Blatchford I (2010). The influence of child, family, home factors and pre-school education on the identification of special educational needs at age 10. *British Educational Research Journal*. UK. University of Bamberg, Department for Education, University of Oxford, Institute of Education & University of London.

Bailey G (2012). Emotional wellbeing for children with special educational needs and disabilities. London. SAGE Publications.

Baker DB, Benjamin J & Ludy T (2000). The affirmation of the scientist practitioner: a look back at Boulder. *American Psychologist*, 55 (2): 241–247.

Bavolek S (2003). The nurturing programme. In Hunt C. *The parenting puzzle: your guide to transforming family life*. Northampton. Alden Group Publishers.

Boxall M & Bennathan M (2014). The Boxall Profile handbook revised. www.nurturegroups.org/publications/lorem-ipsum

Brabban A, McGonagle I & Brooker C (2006). The 10 essential shared capabilities: a framework for mental health practice. *The journal of mental health workforce development*, 1 (3). eprints.lincoln.ac.uk/996/4/Journal_MHTraining2.pdf

Children and Families Act (2014). London. HMSO.

The Children's Society (2011). 4 in every 10 – disabled children living in poverty. www.childrenssociety.org.uk

Children's Workforce Development Council (2010). Refreshing the common core of skills and knowledge. www.cwdcouncil.org.uk/common-core/

Children's Workforce Matters (2015). Common Assessment Framework. www.childrensworkforcematters.org.

uk/workforce-matters/archive/common-assessment-framework/

Coughlan B (2010). Critical issues in the emotional wellbeing of pupils with special educational needs. London. Specialist Schools and Academies Trust.

Daniel B & Wassell S (2003). The school years: assessing and promoting resilience in vulnerable children. London. Jessica Kingsley Publishers.

Davies S (2012). CMO Annual Report: Our Children Deserve Better. www.gov.uk/government/publications/chief-medical-officers-annual-report-2012-our-children-deserve-better-prevention-pays

Department for Children, Schools and Families (2009). Improving the attainment of looked after children in primary schools – guidance for schools. London. DfCSF.

Department for Communities and Local Government (2012). Working with troubled families: a guide to the evidence and good practice. London. Department for Communities and Local Government.

Department for Education (2010). Overview: National Academy for Parenting Research (NAPR). www.kcl.ac.uk/ioppn/depts/cap/research/NAPR/index.aspx

Department for Education (2011). The common assessment framework for children and young people – practitioners guide. http://webarchive.nationalarchives.gov.uk/20130401151715/http://www.education.gov.uk/publications/standard/publicationDetail/Page1/DFES-0337-2006

Department for Education (2012). The impact of pupil behaviour and wellbeing on educational outcomes. www.education.gov.uk/publications/standard/publicationDetail/Page1/DFE-RB253

Department for Education (2014a). Mental health and behaviour in schools: departmental advice for school staff. London. DfE.

Department for Education (2014b). Special educational needs in England, January 2014. www.gov.uk/government/uploads/system/uploads/attachment_data/file/362704/SFR26-2014_SEN_06102014.pdf

Department for Education (2014c). Statutory guidance. National curriculum in England: framework for key stages 1 to 4. London. DfE.

Department for Education and Skills (2001). Promoting children's mental health within early years and school settings. London. HMSO.

Department for Education and Skills (2005a). Primary National Strategy – excellence and enjoyment: social and emotional aspects of learning. London. DfES.

Department for Education and Skills (2005b). School self-evaluation: behaviour and attendance primary electronic audit. The Primary National Strategy. www.standards. dfes.gov.primary/publications/banda/eaudit

Department for Education & Department of Health (2015). Special educational needs and disability (SEND) code of practice and regulations. London. HMSO.

Department of Health (2012). Report of the children and young people's health outcomes forum – mental health sub-group. London. DH.

Department of Health (2014). Closing the gap: priorities for essential change in mental health. London. DH.

Drabble S (2013). Support for children with special educational needs (SEN). RAND Corporation. www. rand.org/content/dam/rand/pubs/research_reports/ RR100/RR180/RAND_RR180.pdf

Emmerson E & Hatton C (2007). The mental health of children and adolescents with learning disabilities in Great Britain. Lancaster. Lancaster Institute for Health Records.

Faulkner J (2011). Class of 2011 yearbook: how happy are young people and why does it matter? Relate. www. relate.org.uk/policy-campaigns/publications/class-2011-yearbook-how-happy-are-young-people-and-why-does-it-matter.

Feeney J & Noller P (1996). Adult attachment. California. Sage Publications.

Goldberg S (2000) Attachment and Development. London. Arnold.

Grotberg E (1997). The international resilience project. In John M (Ed.) *A charge against society: a child's right to protection*. London. Jessica Kingsley Publishers.

GL Assessment (2015). Measures of children's mental health and psychological wellbeing. www.gl-assessment. co.uk/products/measures-childrens-mental-health-psychological-wellbeing/measures-childrens-mental-health

HM Government UK (2007). 2020 Children's Plan, UK: building brighter futures – summary. webarchive. nationalarchives.gov.uk/20130401151715/http://www. education.gov.uk/publications/eOrderingDownload/ Childrens_Plan_Summary.pdf

HM Government UK (2011). No health without mental health: a cross-government mental health outcomes strategy for people of all ages. London. HM Government UK.

Heaven B (2008). Emotional health and wellbeing: teaching to inspire. Optimus Education. www.teachingexpertise. com

Hopwood O & Pharoah R (2012). Families on the front-line – local spending on children's services in austerity. UK. ESRO & Family and Parent Institute.

Howe D, Brandon M, Hinings D & Schofield G (1999).

Attachment Theory, Child Maltreatment and Family Support. London. Macmillan.

Love A & Thompson M (1988). Language disorders and attention deficit disorders in young children referred for psychiatric services: analysis of prevalence and a conceptual synthesis. *American Journal of Orthopsychiatry*, 58: 52–64.

Mansell J (2010). Raising our sights. UK. Mencap. www. mencap.org.uk/raising-our-sights-report

McFall RM (1982). A review and reformulation of the concept of social skills. *Behavioural Assessment*, 4: 1–33.

Mental Health Foundation (2015). How can we help ourselves? www.mentalhealth.org.uk/help-information/ an-introduction-to-mental-health/how-can-we-help-ourselves/

Murphy M & Fonagy P (2012). Annual report of the chief medical officer: our children deserve better. London. DH.

National CAMHS Support Service (2011a). Better mental health outcomes for children and young people – a resource directory for commissioners. www.chimat.org. uk/resource/view.aspx?RID=104048

National CAMHS Support Service (2011b). NCSS National Workforce Programme. The Comprehensive CAMHS Integrated Workforce Planning Tool (IWPT). http:// atlas.chimat.org.uk/IAS/camhs

National Children's Bureau (2012). Beyond the cuts – children's charities adapting to austerity. www.ncb.org. uk/media/705870/beyond_the_cuts.pdf

The National Institute for Health and Care Excellence (2014). Social and emotional wellbeing in primary education. pathways.nice.org.uk/pathways/social-and-emotional-wellbeing-for-children-and-young-people

Office for National Statistics (2004). Mental health of children and young people in Great Britain (2004), summary report. www.hscic.gov.uk/catalogue/ PUB06116/ment-heal-chil-youn-peop-gb-2004-rep2.pdf

Ofsted (2013). Not yet good enough: personal, social, health and economic education in schools. www.ofsted.gov.uk/ resources/130065

Pascal C & Bertram T (1997). Effective early learning. London. Hodder & Stoughton.

PSHE Association (2014). Guidance on developing your PSHE curriculum and programme of study. UK. PSHE Association.

Richter J (1995). NIMH Collaborative multisite multimodal treatment study of children with ADHD. *Journal of American Academy of Children and Adolescent Psychiatry*, 34: 987–1000.

Ridge T (2009). Living with poverty: a review of the literature on children's and families experiences of poverty. London. Department for Work and Pensions.

Rutter M (1985). Resilience in the face of adversity: protective factors and resistance to psychiatric disorder. *British Journal of Psychiatry*, 147: 598–611.

Scott S, Knapp M, Henderson J & Maughan B (2001). Financial cost of social exclusion: follow up study of anti-social children into adulthood. *British Medical Journal*, 323: 191–194.

Seligman M (2011). Flourish: a new understanding of happiness and wellbeing and how to achieve them. London. Nicholas Brealey Publishing.

Skills for Health (2015). Core functions child and adolescent mental health services (Tiers 3 and 4) national workforce programme. www.skillsforhealth.org.uk/resources/service-area/23-child-and-adolescent-mental-health-services-camhs

Werner E (1990). Protective factors and individual resilience. In Meisels SJ & Shonkoff JP (Eds.). *Handbook of early childhood intervention.* Cambridge. Cambridge University Press.

Werner E & Smith R (1992). Overcoming the odds: high risk children from birt0h to adulthood. New York. Cornell University Press.

Wimmer H & Perner J (1983). Beliefs about beliefs: Representation and constraining function of wrong beliefs in young children's understanding standing of deception. *Cognition,* 13: 103–128.

World Health Organisation (2007). Mental health: strengthening mental health promotion. Geneva. WHO.

YoungMinds (2011). Local authorities and CAMHS budgets 2012/2013 briefing report. www.youngminds.org.uk/about/our_campaigns/cuts_to_camhs_services

Youth in Mind (2012). Information for researchers and professionals about the strengths and difficulties questionnaires. www.sdqinfo.org/

NOTES